Clock hours   Dec 1   p.23

How's My Kid Doing?

Thomas R. Guskey

. . . .

How's My Kid Doing?

A Parent's Guide to Grades, Marks, and Report Cards

JOSSEY-BASS
A Wiley Company
www.josseybass.com

Published by Jossey-Bass
A Wiley Imprint
989 Market Street, San Francisco, CA 94103-1741   www.josseybass.com

Note: Some of the material in this book was previously published in *Developing Grading and Reporting Systems for Student Learning,* by Thomas R. Guskey and Jane M. Bailey, Thousand Oaks, CA: Corwin Press, 2001. Copyright © 2001 by Corwin Press, Inc. Reprinted by permission of the publisher.

Jossey-Bass books and products are available through most bookstores. To contact Jossey-Bass directly call our Customer Care Department within the U.S. at (800) 956-7739, outside the U.S. at (317) 572-3986 or fax (317) 572-4002.

Jossey-Bass also publishes its books in a variety of electronic formats. Some content that appears in print may not be available in electronic books.

Library of Congress Cataloging-in-Publication Data

Guskey, Thomas R.
  How's my kid doing? : a parent's guide to grades, marks, and
report cards / Thomas R. Guskey.— 1st ed.
      p. cm. — (The Jossey-Bass education series)
Includes bibliographical references and index.
  ISBN 0-7879-6073-X (alk. paper)
  ISBN 0-7879-6735-1 (paperback)
  1. Grading and marking (Students)—United States. 2. School
reports—United States. I. Title. II. Series.
  LB3060.37 .G89 2002
  372.27'2—dc21

2001006206

Printed in the United States of America
FIRST EDITION
HB Printing   10 9 8 7 6 5 4 3 2 1
PB Printing   10 9 8 7 6 5 4

The Jossey-Bass Education Series

Contents

. . . .

To Jeannie

Preface

Few topics create more problems between parents and educators than grading and reporting. And few problems are more difficult to solve. Parents, students, teachers, and school administrators all seem to agree that we need better grading and reporting systems. Rarely do these different groups agree, however, on what form those new systems should take. Parents want clear and useful information on how their child is doing in school. Teachers want to inform parents about students' academic performance. But mutually satisfying these different wants often proves difficult.

Changes educators have made in grading and reporting in recent years have intensified these problems. Instead of using numerical marks or letter grades, many teachers today report students' learning progress on "grade level standards" and "developmental continuums." Educators believe these new methods provide parents with better and more descriptive information than do letter grades and traditional report cards. But many parents find these new methods confusing and unclear. Even those who understand the new forms have a hard time figuring out the adequacy of their child's performance or whether it's in line with the teacher's expectations. That's why, after reviewing a newly developed reporting form, they frequently turn to the teacher and ask, "So, how's my kid doing?"

To get a better understanding of their perspectives on grading and reporting, several colleagues and I conducted a series of surveys and informal interviews with groups of parents. It's not surprising that we learned that most parents' ideas about grading come from their own past experiences in school. They recall how their teachers recorded percentages and letter grades on everything from homework assignments and reports to quizzes and major examinations. Regardless of how subjective these marks may have been, their meaning seemed clear and concise. They conveyed the teachers' judgments about how students were doing, whether or not they measured up, and where they stood in comparison to their classmates.

That same kind of clear and concise information is what parents want today. Most told us they want honest and detailed information from teachers about how their child is doing in school. But they also want that information in an easy-to-understand form that makes sense. If their child isn't doing well, they want specific suggestions from educators about what can be done to help. Rather than simply documenting students' achievement or performance, parents see grading and reporting as a challenge in effective communication.

And that's precisely the purpose of this book: to help both parents and educators meet that challenge. Educators need to understand parents' perspectives on grading and reporting. But parents and guardians also have to understand what's involved in grading and reporting so that they can become better partners with educators in efforts to improve these procedures.

Specifically, this book is designed to help parents (1) recognize the different purposes of grading and reporting, (2) identify the advantages and shortcomings of various grading and reporting methods, (3) understand the elements of an effective reporting system, and (4) appreciate the challenges teachers face in developing fair, accurate, and equitable grading policies and practices. By emphasizing the qualities of effective communication, I also hope to show how parents and educators can break down the communication barriers between schools and homes, and cooperate in their efforts to help all children learn.

Today we know a lot about the effectiveness of various grading and reporting policies and practices. We also know what doesn't work and what may be potentially harmful to students. This knowledge offers us clear direction for improvement efforts. But if these efforts are to succeed, parents and educators have to work together as partners. They have to understand each other's perspectives and then collaborate to make things better. I hope that this book will help in that important process.

Acknowledgments

> A hundred times every day I remind myself that my inner and outer life are based on the labors of others.
>
> *Albert Einstein*

Although my name appears alone on the cover of this book, many people contributed mightily to the work and ideas presented on these pages. Without their help and unselfish assistance, this book never would have been possible.

First is my friend and the editor of this book, Lesley Iura. Lesley had confidence in this project when many others did not, and worked hard to see it completed. Her energy and support were constant and greatly appreciated.

Second is another friend and colleague, Jane Bailey, director of teaching and learning for the Petoskey Public Schools in Petoskey, Michigan. Jane and I worked together on two earlier books, *Developing Grading and Reporting Systems for Student Learning* (Guskey and Bailey, 2001) and *Implementing Student-Led Conferences* (Bailey and Guskey, 2001), from which many of the ideas presented here were drawn. Jane also reviewed early versions of this book and offered many helpful suggestions. Her insights and thoughtful criticism made it a much better book.

I'm also indebted to my friends at Corwin Press, especially President Gracia Alkiema and Education Editor Rachel Livsey. They graciously allowed me to take ideas presented in earlier works prepared for education leaders and translate them into this work designed for parents. Their cooperation and support were instrumental in the development of this book.

Evident throughout this work is the influence of the many students, parents, teachers, administrators, and other leaders with whom I've worked over the last decade on grading issues. They faithfully reminded me that the best ideas are always simple and practical.

Perhaps most of all I'm indebted to my family and special friends. I have the great advantage in my life to be surrounded by wonderful people who stand by me in times of trouble, endure my fits of impatience, show me kindness when I am truly undeserving, and help keep my work and life in perspective. They are the best evidence to show that it's not what, but who you have in your life that really counts. Without their love and understanding, neither this book nor any other work would have been possible.

February 2002   Thomas R. Guskey
                                                       Lexington, Kentucky

How's My Kid Doing?

· ·

1

Getting Started

To address any problem you must first be able to talk about it. So the purpose of this first chapter is to clarify terms, identify purposes, and describe developments that have led to recent changes in grading and reporting. With a common knowledge base and shared vocabulary, parents and educators will be better prepared to communicate about grading and reporting, and then cooperate in improvement efforts.

What Do We Mean by Grading and Reporting?

Although people hold widely varying views about grading, most agree that it's essentially an exercise in professional judgment on the part of teachers. Grading involves the collection and evaluation of evidence on students' achievement or performance. Sometimes this evidence comes from a single demonstration of learning. For example, a teacher might evaluate students' performance on a single assignment, quiz, oral report, or composition. At other times grading involves teachers' summary judgments of a collection of evidence on student learning drawn from several sources over an extended period of time. This time period is usually referred to as a "grading period" and may be six weeks, nine weeks, an academic semester, or an entire school year.

Teachers generally express the results of their evaluative judgments of students' performance in terms of grades or marks. Although some educators distinguish between "grades" and "marks" (see, for example, O'Connor, 1999), most consider these terms synonymous. Both imply a set of symbols, words, or numbers used to designate different levels of performance. They might be letter grades such as A, B, C, D, and F; symbols such as ✔+, ✔, ✔−; descriptive words such as Exemplary, Satisfactory, and Needs Improvement; or numerals such 4, 3, 2, and 1.

In assigning grades teachers must determine the criteria for each category or level of performance. In other words, they must specify the difference between an A B, C, D, and F; between ✔+, ✔, and ✔−; and so on. Some teachers have clear descriptions of performance that they use to differentiate various levels. These are referred to as "criterion-referenced" standards and can be communicated to students prior to an assessment of learning. Other teachers simply compare each student's performance to that of the other students in the group or class. These are referred to as "norm-referenced" standards or more familiarly as grading "on the curve." Because norm-referenced standards are based on how well other students perform, they cannot be specified prior to an assessment of learning, but only after assessment results are tallied. Grading "on the curve" is discussed in more detail in Chapter Three.

Reporting, then, is the process by which these judgments of students' performance are communicated to parents, students, or others. The most obvious method for such communication is the report card. But educators have a variety of methods to communicate information on student learning. Examples include newsletters, weekly or monthly progress reports, phone calls, evaluated projects or assignments, parent-teacher conferences, and student-led conferences.

Are Grading and Reporting Essential?

Although grading and reporting serve a vital role in education, they're not essential to teaching or to learning. In other words, teachers don't need grades or reporting forms to teach well, and students don't need them in order to learn (Frisbie and Waltman, 1992). .

For teaching and learning to be effective, however, teachers need to check regularly on how students are doing. They need to find out who's learning well, who's not, and what particular problems or difficulties students are experiencing. But *checking* is different from *grading*. Checking involves gathering evidence in order to guide improvements. Grading involves judging students' competence and evaluating the merits of their performance at a specific time. So while teachers use checking to *diagnose* and *prescribe*, they use grading to *evaluate* and *describe* (Bloom, Madaus, and Hastings, 1981).

The same evidence can sometimes be used for checking or for grading, but seldom can it be used for both. One teacher, for example, might administer a brief quiz as a checking device or "formative" assessment. Results from this quiz "count," in that there are consequences based on students' performance. However, instead of being a part of students' grades, results are used to find out which students have learned particular concepts well and which students need additional time and study. The quiz is then followed by corrective instruction for students who need additional assistance and by enrichment activities to extend the learning of students who demonstrate their mastery of the concepts (see Guskey, 1997).

Another teacher might use the same quiz as a "summative" assessment to judge how well students have learned those specific concepts. Results are not used to guide further instruction. Instead, they are recorded in a grade book and then used in calculating course grades. Individual teachers usually decide whether a particular source of evidence will be used for checking or for grading.

Because most teachers do both checking and grading, they're compelled to be both advocates as well as judges of their students—roles that are not necessarily complimentary (Bishop, 1992). Finding a meaningful compromise between these dual roles makes many teachers uncomfortable, especially those who teach in the early elementary grades (Barnes, 1985).

Why Are Educators Changing Their Grading and Reporting Methods?

Developments That Have Prompted Change
in Grading and Reporting Systems

1. Recognition of inconsistencies in the grading policies and practices of elementary, middle, and high school educators shows the need for change.

2. The growing emphasis on standards and performance assessments makes current reporting practices inadequate.

3. Advanced technology allows for more efficient reporting of detailed information on student learning.

4. Growing awareness of the gap between our knowledge of grading and reporting methods and common practice necessitates change.

Four different but interrelated developments have prompted educators to change their grading and reporting methods (see the box above). First is recognition of inconsistencies in grading policies and practices across the elementary, middle, and high school levels. Educators and parents alike recognize that as students move from one level of education to the next, grading and reporting practices often change drastically. Grading policies, grading criteria, and reporting methods all change, as do the form and structure of report cards. While some of these changes are due to differences in instruction, others are the result of poor communication among educators across the different levels. To resolve these inconsistencies and bring greater clarity to grading procedures, educators have begun to collaborate across levels and to work with parents to revise grading and reporting methods.

A second development is the growing emphasis on educational standards and performance assessments. Educators today are no longer satisfied with instruction that focuses on only basic skills. Instead they want students to engage in "authentic" problem-solving tasks that require them to think, plan, analyze, integrate, and construct. In developing learning standards that emphasize these skills and devising assessments that measure how well students can perform them, educators discovered that their traditional marking systems were inadequate and obsolete. This, in turn, prompted calls for the development of better and more appropriate reporting methods.

The third development that spurred this effort is advanced technology. Modern technology allows educators to record and share vast amounts of detailed information on student learning. These developments also make it possible to do things that were unimaginable in the past. For example, the same technology that allows supermarkets to itemize every purchase on an individualized charge slip, and permits businesses to provide individualized billings for items bought at locations throughout the world, can be used to produce individualized report cards that show what students are working on and what progress they have made on a daily basis.

Fourth, and perhaps most important, is increased awareness of the large gap between our knowledge of grading and reporting methods and what is common practice. Despite the fact that grading and reporting have been the subject of innumerable studies, current practices tend to be based more on tradition and opinion than on a thoughtful analysis of this growing body of evidence. Too often practices are continued simply because "We've always done it that way," or because "That's the way our teachers did it." While researchers have confirmed that some of the grading and reporting practices used by teachers in the past were sound, others clearly were not. To make progress and to benefit students, we must do our best to ensure this extensive knowledge on grading and reporting is used to guide current practice.

What Are the Purposes of Grading and Reporting?

If grading and reporting are not essential to teaching and learning, then what purposes do they serve? Researchers have asked educators this question and generally find that their answers can be classified in six broad categories (see Feldmesser, 1971; Frisbie and Waltman, 1992; Linn, 1983). The major purposes they identify include

1. *To communicate the achievement status of students to parents and others.* Grading and reporting provide parents and others (for example, guardians) with information about their child's progress in school. They also serve to involve parents in educational processes.

2. *To provide information students can use for self-evaluation.* Grading and reporting offer students information about the level or adequacy of their academic achievement and performance in school.

3. *To select, identify, or group students for certain educational paths or programs.* Grades are a primary source of information used to select students for special programs. High grades are typically required for entry into gifted education programs, while low grades are often the first indicator of learning problems

that result in students' placement in special needs programs. Grades are also used as a criterion for entry into colleges and universities.

4. *To provide incentives for students to learn.* Although some may debate the idea, extensive evidence shows that grades and other reporting methods are important factors in determining the amount of effort students put forth and how seriously they regard any assignment or assessment task (Cameron and Pierce, 1994, 1996; Chastain, 1990; Ebel, 1979).

5. *To evaluate the effectiveness of instructional programs.* Comparisons of grade distributions and other reporting evidence are frequently used to judge the value or effectiveness of new programs and instructional techniques.

6. *To provide evidence of students' lack of effort or inappropriate responsibility.* Grades and other reporting devices are frequently used to document unsuitable behaviors on the part of students, and some teachers threaten students with poor grades to coerce more acceptable behavior.

Although all of these purposes may be legitimate, educators seldom agree on which purpose is most important. And that's precisely the problem. Because they don't agree on what purpose is most important, educators often attempt to address *all* of these purposes with a single reporting device, usually a report card, and typically end up achieving no purpose very well (Austin and McCann, 1992). The simple truth is that no single reporting device can serve all of these purposes well. In fact, some purposes are actually counter to others.

Suppose, for example, that the educators in a particular school strive to have all students learn well. Suppose, too, that they are highly successful in their efforts and, as a result, nearly all of their students attain high levels of achievement and earn high grades. These results pose no problem if the purpose of grading and reporting is to communicate students' achievement status to parents or to provide students with self-evaluation information. The educators from this school can be proud of what they've accomplished and can look forward to sharing those results with parents, students, and others.

This same outcome poses major problems, however, if the purpose of grading and reporting is to select students for special educational paths or to evaluate the effectiveness of instructional programs. Selection and evaluation demand variation in the grades. They require that the grades be dispersed across all possible categories in order to differentiate among students and programs. How else can selection take place or one program be judged better than another? But if all students learn well and earn the same high grades, there's no variation. Determining differences under such conditions is impossible. Thus while one purpose is served very well, another purpose is not.

That's why reform efforts to improve grading and reporting must begin with broad-based discussions about purpose. Participants in these discussions need to decide what message is to be communicated through grading and reporting, who is the audience or audiences for that message, and what is the intended goal of the communication. Once decisions about purpose are made, other critical issues about reporting methods and forms are much easier to address and resolve.

Why Should We Develop a Reporting System?

Since no single reporting device can serve all purposes well, improvement efforts must focus on developing a *reporting system* that includes a variety of reporting tools. Each tool within such a system should be designed to communicate specific information to a particular audience in an appropriate format. Reporting reforms that fail usually attempt to accomplish too many purposes with a single reporting device or expect that device to serve purposes for which it is ill-suited (Allison and Friedman, 1995; Pardini, 1997). A reporting system that includes multiple reporting tools, however, can be adapted to meet a variety of diverse reporting needs.

A particular school's reporting system might include a report card, standardized assessment reports, planned phone calls to parents, monthly progress reports, school open-houses, newsletters to parents, portfolios or exhibits of student' work, and regularly scheduled student-led conferences. Each of these reporting tools might have a different purpose that would guide its development, establish its form or structure, and determine the criteria by which its effectiveness is judged.

Parents generally favor the use of reporting systems. Although some evidence indicates that most parents would like to receive report cards more frequently (J. F. Wemette, personal communication, 1994), our surveys and interviews with parents show this may not be completely accurate. We found instead that parents simply want more regular information from educators about how their child is doing in school. A reporting system that includes multiple reporting tools can address this concern and, if well designed, can offer parents precisely the kind of information they want and need.

The accompanying box lists some of the reporting tools frequently included in schools' reporting systems. Each is described more thoroughly in Chapter Six.

How Do We Develop a Reporting System?

The first issue that needs to be addressed in putting together a reporting system is the primary purpose of each included reporting tool (see box on page 10). Educators sometimes become enamored with a particular reporting tool and move ahead in its development without carefully considering the purpose. They start off saying "Let's change our report card," or "Let's have students develop portfolios," without ever considering why they are doing it or what purpose they hope to accomplish. But in reporting, just as in architecture, form must always follow function. In other words, purpose must always precede method or format. Decisions about purpose must always come first.

Tools That Might Be Included in a
Comprehensive Reporting System

Report cards	Evaluated projects or assignments
Notes attached to report cards	Portfolios or exhibits of students' work
Standardized assessment reports	Homework assignments
Phone calls to parents	Homework hotlines
Weekly or monthly progress reports	School Web pages
School open-houses	Parent-teacher conferences
Newsletters to parents	Student-teacher conferences
Personal letters to parents	Student-led conferences

If, for example, it's decided that the primary purpose of the report card is to communicate information to parents about students' achievement or performance, then parents must be able to understand that information, interpret it correctly, and make appropriate use of it. This means that parents should be involved in the development of the report card and should be given opportunities to offer suggestions and feedback on its implementation. If the report card is too complex for parents to understand, or if it offers information they cannot interpret, then that report card has failed its purpose.

Similarly, if it's decided that the primary purpose of the report card is to provide information to students that they can use for self-evaluation, then students should be involved in the development and implementation of the report card. Not only must they understand the information on the report card, they also need guidance and direction on how to use that information. If the information is ambiguous to students or nonprescriptive, again the report card hasn't served its intended purpose.

How Do We Clarify the Purpose of Each Reporting Tool?

To make clear the intended purpose of each reporting tool, that purpose should be written directly on the tool itself. The purpose of the report card, for example, should be clearly printed on the card for everyone to see. Similarly, the purpose of a monthly progress report or a school newsletter should be stated on the top of that form. Even student portfolios should include a statement of purpose printed on the portfolio cover or in an introductory statement prepared collaboratively by teachers and students. Although different reporting tools can serve different purposes, an explicit statement of each tool's purpose helps clarify its intent, the information it includes, and the intended audience. Miscommunication and misinterpretation are far less likely when the purpose of each tool is clearly spelled out.

Statements of purpose vary as widely as the reporting tools themselves. A highlighted box on the front of the report card might include a statement such as the following:

> The purpose of this report card is to describe students' learning progress to their parents and others, based on our school's learning expectations for each grade level. It is intended to inform parents about learning successes and to guide improvements when needed.

This statement tells the specific aim of the report card, for whom the information is intended, and how that information might be used. The purpose of a newsletter for parents, on the other hand, might be stated as follows:

> The purpose of this newsletter is to inform parents of the topics students will be exploring during the next month, the learning activities we have planned, and how those activities can be supported at home.

The most appropriate set of reporting tools to include in a reporting system will vary depending on the context. Differences from grade to grade are also not uncommon. In most cases elementary reporting systems differ from middle school and high school systems. At all levels, however, the purpose of each tool should be clear to everyone involved in the grading and reporting process: teachers, parents, students, and administrators.

Summary

Grading is an exercise in professional judgment on the part of teachers that involves the collection and evaluation of evidence on students' achievement or performance. The results of teachers' evaluative judgments are typically expressed in terms of grades or marks that designate different levels of performance. Reporting is the process by which these judgments are communicated to parents, students, or others.

Although grading and reporting are not essential to teaching or learning, they do serve several vital purposes. Because no single reporting device can accomplish all of these purposes, however, reform efforts should focus on the development of a comprehensive reporting system. Such a system will include multiple reporting tools, each designed to communicate specific information to a particular audience for a well-defined purpose.

2

Perceptions and Responsibilities

To make improvements, we first have to understand the perceptions of those involved. So in this chapter we turn to parents', teachers', and students' perceptions of grading and reporting. We'll also consider the responsibilities of each of these groups in the grading and reporting process, and how they usually go about fulfilling those responsibilities.

Parents' Perceptions of Grading and Reporting

As I described in Chapter One, parents' perceptions of grading and reporting are based largely on their experiences as students. And in most cases, those experiences involved percentages and letter grades. Parents know these grading methods, and they make sense to parents. That's also why most parents view departures from these methods with some skepticism. Still, when we asked what changes in grading and reporting they would like to see, parents most frequently mentioned three ideas.

First, the majority told us that they would like to receive *more regular information* about their child's learning progress in school. When asked about report cards, for example, most parents indicated they would like to receive them every six weeks rather than every nine weeks. This runs counter to the desires of most teachers, of course, who find completing report cards every nine weeks challenging enough. When we pressed this issue in our interviews, however, we discovered that parents don't necessarily want report cards more often. Instead, they simply want information from educators about how their child is doing on a more regular basis.

Second, parents said they want *more detailed information* about how their child is doing in school. They were quick to add, however, that they want this information in a jargon-free form that they understand (see Million, 1999). This probably explains parents' preferences for letter grades. It's not that they're convinced of the merits of letter grades in comparison to other reporting methods. Rather, they received letter grades during their school years and believe they understand what letter grades mean. To parents, letter grades possess two highly desirable qualities: they communicate information efficiently and they are easy to interpret.

We also discovered that many parents' apprehensions about new reporting methods stem from confusion over the terms educators use. Certain words and phrases that educators believe are clear and precise are either mysterious or meaningless to parents. In some cases this causes parents to misinterpret completely what educators want to communicate.

The word *emerging*, for example, is used in many reporting forms to describe a skill or understanding that students have just begun to develop. Many parents, however, find this word needlessly complex. When we suggested that *emerging* simply meant "beginning," several parents responded, "If you mean 'beginning,' why don't you just say 'beginning'?"

Similarly, many teachers use the phrase "developmentally appropriate" to describe activities that are well suited to students' level of cognitive, physical, and emotional maturity (Galen, 1994). Many parents, however, interpret *developmental* to mean "remedial." They equate such activities with those offered in "developmental" courses in high schools and colleges where the label "developmental" is attached to the remedial work students must complete before they can be considered "on level" or "on track." To many parents, there-fore, a child engaged in "developmentally appropriate" activities is in serious trouble and at risk of failure—clearly not the message teachers want to convey.

The third thing parents revealed is that they need practical sug-gestions about how they can help their children. Most parents dearly love their children and sincerely want them to succeed in school (see Henderson and Berla, 1995). At the same time, how-ever, they're uncertain about teachers' specific expectations and what they can do at home to help (Hoover-Dempsey and Sandler, 1997). This kind of information is extremely important to parents but frequently neglected or ignored by educators (Cattermole and Robinson, 1985; Kreider and Lopez, 1999).

Finally, we learned that many parents welcome the opportunity to become involved in reforming grading and reporting. Their help is especially valuable, too, in designing programs to inform parents about changes in grading policies or procedures. Such programs help parents understand the reasons behind recommended changes in grading, as well as the advantages of the new reporting tools to be included in a revised reporting system. The best of these programs show parents how to interpret and use reported information to help children improve their performance in school.

Changes in Grading and Reporting
Recommended by Parents

1. Provide more regular information about their child's learning progress.

2. Offer more detailed information about how well their child is doing in school.

3. Make specific, practical suggestions on how they can help their child at home.

Parents' Perceptions of Teachers

As part of our discussion with parents we also asked, "What do you most want to know about your child's teacher?" and "What teacher characteristics or traits are most important to you?" Although parents' answers varied slightly, depending on whether their child was enrolled in elementary or secondary school, overall they were surprisingly consistent.

Two items top the list of things parents want to know about their child's teacher. First, they want to know that *the teacher is competent.* They want to be assured that their child's teacher is well trained, knowledgeable, and well prepared to teach (Million, 1999). They also stressed, however, that they don't want a "know-it-all, unapproachable clinician." Instead, they want their child's teacher to be capable and highly skilled, yet personable (see Rich, 1998). Although a few parents expressed reservations about having their child placed in the classroom of a beginning teacher, most indicated that years of teaching experience matter little to them.

Second, and equally important, parents want to know that *the teacher cares about their child as an individual.* They hope the teacher will take the time to know their child as a person and in doing so will recognize their child's positive attributes as well as the faults. Most parents see their child as a special and highly unique individual, and they want their child's teacher to share that perception (see Watts, 1996).

What Parents Most Want to Know
About Their Child's Teacher

1. The teacher is competent.

2. The teacher cares about their child as an individual.

Teachers' Perceptions of Grading and Reporting

Teachers' perceptions of grading and reporting tend to vary depending on their teaching level. Elementary teachers typically express frustration with the entire grading process. They recognize the need to provide parents with information about the achievement and performance of their children but see the evaluative aspects of grading as counter to their roles as teachers. Most elementary teachers want to be advocates for their students, but grading requires them to be judges.

Secondary teachers, on the other hand, usually respond to questions about grading by opening their grade book—a large, spiral-bound notebook of meticulously kept records on students' performance. Today many middle and high school teachers use electronic grade books to record this information on computer spreadsheets. Each page of their grade book lists the names of the students in each of their classes, followed by columns filled with a complicated array of numbers and symbols. At the end of each marking period, they combine this information by using complex mathematical formulae that incorporate percentages, weighted averages, and different point-tallying options. With the aid of a calculator or computer, they calculate a summary number to the one hundred-thousandth decimal point that they then convert to a corresponding letter grade.

When asked about why they grade, the responses of elementary and secondary teachers are more similar. Elementary teachers generally claim that they have to because parents and administrators demand it. Secondary teachers also mention parents' demands and often point to college and university admission requirements. Nearly all teachers admit, however, that they really don't like grading and reporting. They describe the process as troublesome, time-consuming, and counter to what they consider to be their major responsibilities as teachers; that is, to engage students in high-quality learning experiences. Many indicate that they would like to get rid of grading completely or at least have a more efficient reporting system that would complement their instructional responsibilities rather than detract from them.

Sources of Teachers' Grading and Reporting Practices

When we asked how they developed their grading policies and practices, both elementary and secondary teachers described a combination of four sources of influence. First and foremost they refer to their experiences as students. In other words, they do what was done to them. From the wide array of grading policies and practices their teachers used, they select those that they believe were fairest, worked best, and were most appropriate.

A second important influence on teachers' grading and reporting practices is their personal philosophies of teaching and learning (Barnes, Bull, Perry, and Campbell, 1998; Frisbie and Waltman, 1992). Some teachers believe their purpose in teaching is to differentiate students according to their talent level, ranging from those with exceptional ability and skill to those who may need specialized assistance. Other teachers object to this sorting and selecting function, and insist that their major purpose is to develop talent and foster personal growth in all students.

These different philosophies typically translate into very different grading policies and practices. The first group of teachers is likely to emphasize the evaluative nature of grading and the use of grades to recognize excellence in the performance of a few students. The second group of teachers will stress the information and communication functions of reporting and how it can be used to facilitate the learning process.

The third source of information from which teachers draw is district, building, department, or grade-level grading policies. A recent nationwide survey found that about two-thirds of all schools have established policies on grading (Polloway and others, 1994). Unfortunately, majorities of teachers describe these policies as ambiguous and unclear, and stress they had little or no role in developing them. Nevertheless, teachers at all levels generally feel compelled to follow these policies and make adaptations only when they are convinced that such changes are both legally and educationally defensible.

The final factor that influences teachers' grading and reporting practices is what they learned in their teacher preparation programs. Unfortunately, discussions about grading are typically restricted to a single class session in an educational psychology course (Stiggins, 1993). Still, these discussions provide prospective teachers with the opportunity to explore a few relevant grading issues.

Because the influence of these four sources on teachers is uneven and inconsistent, teachers' personal grading and reporting practices tend to vary widely, even among teachers in the same school or in the same academic department. This puts students in the difficult position of having to learn a new set of grading policies and rules in every class. Although some students become highly skilled at deciphering these differences, understanding the consequences, and manipulating each system to their advantage, others remain painfully unaware and confused, sometimes suffering tragic results.

Sources of Teachers' Grading Practices

1. The policies and practices they experienced as students.

2. Their personal philosophies of teaching and learning.

3. District, building, department, or grade-level policies on grading and reporting.

4. What they learned about grading and reporting in their undergraduate teacher preparation programs.

Students' Perceptions of Grading and Reporting

Students' experiences with assessment date back to their earliest childhood years, when their parents and other adults appraised their behavior and offered immediate feedback. Appropriate behaviors were encouraged with praise while inappropriate or potentially harmful behaviors met with reprimand or punishment. Parents say things like, "Good job, Christopher!" and "That's right, Jennifer!" to communicate their approval and, "No, no, Elizabeth!" or "Don't do that, Robert!" to let children know their behaviors are not permissible and need to be altered.

When children enter school, their experiences with assessments become more formalized. In the elementary grades, teachers still offer verbal feedback to students based on the results of assessments, often with specific directions for correction when needed. But teachers also must communicate the results of these assessments to parents. Because it's impossible and impractical to share the results from *all* their observations and appraisals, teachers have to condense this information into an overall summary of each student's performance. These summaries are then communicated to parents through marks or grades on a report card or reporting form.

Around the middle school years and sometimes earlier, students' perceptions of grades begin to change, probably due to teachers' shifting emphasis from the information or "formative" aspects of grades to their summative functions. Students no longer see grades as a source of feedback to guide improvements in their learning. Instead they regard grades as the major product that teachers offer in exchange for their performance. This change brings a slow but steady shift in students' focus away from learning and toward what they must do to obtain the particular product they want.

For those who are successful in acquiring a high-level product, the grade takes on great value. These students work hard to obtain their grade and take pride in what they attain. Those who are less successful protect their self-images from guilt by attaching less importance to the product. Some may even consider it insignificant or irrelevant. This change in students' perceptions is reflected in the questions that they ask on entering a class. Instead of inquiring, "What are we going to study?" or "What will I learn?" students are more likely to ask, "What must I do to get a high grade?"

The principal currency used to obtain this product, of course, is points. Over the course of a marking period, almost everything students do in class has a point-value attached to it. Quizzes, tests, projects, laboratory experiments, and homework assignments all represent opportunities for students to earn points (Feldman, Kropf, and Alibrand, 1996). The number of points the teacher assigns to a particular activity determines its value. That is why, for example, when the teacher announces an upcoming project or event, students' first questions are, "Does it count?" and "How many points is it worth?" How teachers answer these questions gives students a clear idea of how much importance they should attach to that particular event.

The Points-Driven Academic Economy of Classrooms

From middle school on, the currency of points dominates the academic economy of classrooms. Students begin to view academic wealth as the number of points they can accumulate. Teachers set the currency exchange rate when they establish their grading standards. Bright students keep track of current exchange rates, calculating far in advance the exact number of points they need to get the grade they want, and adjust their efforts accordingly. They must plan cautiously, knowing that they can lose points or be fined for certain transgressions, such as not completing a homework assignment or turning in a project late. They also pay attention to special events that allow them to earn extra points or bonuses, such as doing an extra project or volunteering for work outside of class.

Students also learn that their grade can be influenced by actions other than their actual academic performance. Their behavior in class, the effort they appear to be making, their politeness in interacting with the teacher, the neatness of their work, and even their appearance can affect their grade. This is sometimes labeled the Eddie Haskell Effect (Guskey and Bailey, 2001), referring to the manipulative antics of a character from the 1960s television show, *Leave It to Beaver*, reruns of which now air in syndication. Though points are clearly important, clever students recognize that these other factors can be crucial in attaining the grade they want.

Students who accumulate large numbers of points and attain high grades earn distinctive labels such as "gifted" or "talented." Their accumulated academic wealth allows them to qualify for special "honors" or "accelerated" classes. Students who acquire few points and are assigned low grades typically are referred for further evaluation. This, in turn, often leads to them being assigned special titles such as "slow learner" or "learning disabled." Although some may dispute this practice, it's well established that high grades are considered a prerequisite to "academically talented" programs, whereas failing grades are the first diagnostic step in the identification of students who are learning disabled (Hargis, 1990).

This emphasis on earning points in order to obtain a particular grade unfortunately diminishes the value of learning. Students are drawn into a points-driven, academic economy system that detracts from education's true purpose. What was originally designed to be a means of summarizing appraisals of student learning becomes an end in itself. Rigid adherence to points-driven systems may appear to bring objectivity and precision to the grading process. But as we will see in later chapters, this objectivity and precision are far more imaginary than real. In the long run, such systems detract from the central purposes of teaching and learning.

Of course, the emphasis on points is not an immutable characteristic of grading and reporting systems, as some might suggest. It stems, instead, from the procedures used in determining grades and how those grades are then used or misused. Thoughtfully designed grading and reporting systems that emphasize the formative and communicative aspects of grades can maintain students' focus on important learning goals. Such systems can actually serve to enhance instructional processes. Especially when combined with other more descriptive information within a comprehensive reporting system, grades can communicate information that is accurate, meaningful, and constructive (Guskey, 1993).

Summary

Perceptions of grading and reporting vary widely among parents, students, and teachers. To fulfill the primary communication purposes of grading and reporting, these drastic differences must be addressed and resolved. Comprehensive reporting systems that include a collection of reporting tools to satisfy the diverse information needs of parents, students, teachers, and others offer the best and most practical solution to these challenging communication problems.

· ·

3

Challenges for Teachers in Grading and Reporting

Regardless of how they feel about grading and reporting, teachers at all levels are required to evaluate students' performance and to report the results of those evaluations to parents, students, and others. Understanding the challenges this imposes on teachers is essential to improving the process. In this chapter we'll explore those challenges and describe how teachers deal with them in their efforts to develop grading policies and practices that are accurate, honest, and fair.

Limiting Subjectivity in Grading

One of the most pressing challenges for teachers in grading and reporting is to limit the negative influence of personal subjectivity. As described in Chapter One, grading is basically an exercise in professional judgment that involves one person (a teacher) making evaluative decisions about the performance of another person (a student). As such, it's an inherently subjective process. Even in schools with specific grading policies, individual teachers usually have great latitude in deciding what counts as part of the grade, how each of those elements will be evaluated or scored, and how those scores will be combined in determining the grade. In most instances teachers also choose how they will assess students' learning, how rigorous or challenging those assessments will be, and the level of performance expected for each grade category. Though communicating these decisions to students may help them understand the teacher's grading procedures, it doesn't make the process of grading any less subjective.

Confounding matters further is that the more detailed grading procedures become, the more likely subjectivity will influence the results (Ornstein, 1994). Highly detailed grading procedures simply allow more opportunities for the unique personal opinions of individual teachers to come into play. The details one teacher focuses on might be different from the details another teacher chooses to emphasize. That's why, for example, general or "holistic" scoring procedures that require teachers to make broad, overall judgments of students' performance are generally more reliable than detailed, analytic procedures. Reliability, in this sense, refers to consistency or agreement in the judgments of different teachers. Two equally skilled teachers typically find it easier to agree on the general classification of a student's performance as Excellent, Fair, or Poor, than they do in their judgments of each specific aspect of that performance.

Balancing Instructional Concerns with Grading Requirements

At the same time, most teachers recognize that detailed and analytic grading procedures are much more helpful to students (Bloom, Madaus, and Hastings, 1981). General or holistic scoring provides students with little guidance on how they can improve their performance. The same is true of a single grade written at the top of students' papers. To make improvements, students need detailed information from the teacher, paired with specific suggestions for correction (Guskey, 1997). The challenge for teachers, therefore, is to find meaningful ways to balance these vital instructional purposes with reporting requirements.

It's also important to keep in mind that subjectivity in grading and reporting isn't always bad. Being subjective doesn't mean that grades lack credibility or are indefensible. Because teachers know their students, understand various dimensions of students' work, and have clear notions of the progress made, their subjective perceptions can yield very accurate descriptions of what students have learned (Brookhart, 1993; O'Donnell and Woolfolk, 1991).

The key to limiting the negative aspects of subjectivity is to recognize that grading is not a simple mechanical process. And as we'll see in later chapters, neither is it a process that can be made more objective with mathematical precision or through the use of computer technology. Teachers at all levels must be clear about their grading standards, the elements they include in determining grades, and how they plan to evaluate those elements. But even with clear standards and grading criteria in place, the process of grading still involves thoughtful, reasonable, but imperfect human judgment. That's why it's so important for parents and teachers to work together to ensure their communication is clear, concise, and well understood by everyone involved in the process.

Establishing Grading Criteria: Norm-Referenced Versus Criterion-Referenced Criteria

Another challenge many teachers face is determining whether their grading standards will be norm-referenced or criterion referenced. As described in Chapter One, norm-referenced standards involve comparing each student's performance to that of other students in the group or class. This is also referred to familiarly as "grading on the curve." Criterion-referenced standards, however, involve the use of clearly stated descriptions of performance that differentiate various levels of quality. Although opinions differ as to which of these two types of standards is better, strong research evidence shows that classroom grading and reporting should *always* be done in reference to specific learning criteria rather than in reference to normative criteria or "on the curve."

In using norm-referenced grading standards, teachers first rank order students in terms of some measure of their achievement or performance. A set percentage of top-ranked students, usually 10 to 20 percent, is assigned the highest grade. A next set percentage, perhaps 20 to 30 percent, is assigned the second highest grade, and so on. The percentages used typically correspond to an approximation of the bell-shaped, normal probability curve; hence, the label "grading on the curve."

Using the normal probability curve as a basis for assigning grades yields highly consistent grade distributions from one teacher to the next. In other words, each teacher's classes have the same percentage of A's, B's, C's, and so on. But as we will see in Chapter Five, this practice has numerous negative consequences. Plus grading "on the curve" communicates nothing about what students have learned or are able to do. It tells only a student's relative standing among classmates, based on what are often ill-defined criteria. Students who receive the high grades might actually have performed very poorly, but simply less poorly than their classmates. Differences between grades are difficult to interpret at best, and meaningless at worst (Bracey, 1994).

Grading standards therefore should always be criterion referenced. This means that teachers at all levels must identify what they want their students to learn, what evidence they will use to verify that learning, and what criteria will be used to judge that evidence. Grades based on clearly stated learning criteria have direct meaning and serve well the communication purposes for which they're intended.

Clarifying Learning Criteria

When grading and reporting relate to learning criteria, teachers are able to provide a clear picture of what students have learned and are able to do. Students and teachers both prefer this approach because they consider it fairer and more equitable (Kovas, 1993). But clarifying learning criteria presents teachers with yet another challenge because so many different types of criteria can be used. The learning criteria teachers use for grading and reporting generally fall into in three broad categories. These include *product, process,* and *progress* criteria.

Product Criteria

Product learning criteria relate to students' specific achievements or level of performance. In other words, they focus on *what* students know and are able to do at a particular point in time. Advocates of standards-based approaches to teaching and learning generally favor product criteria. Teachers who use product criteria often base students' grades or reports exclusively on final examination scores, final products (reports or projects), overall assessments, and other culminating demonstrations of learning.

Process Criteria

Process learning criteria relate not to the final results but to how students got there. They are favored by educators who believe product criteria don't provide a complete picture of student learning. Teachers who consider students' effort or work habits when reporting are using process criteria. So are teachers who count regular classroom quizzes, homework, class participation, or attendance.

Progress Criteria

Progress learning criteria relate to how much students actually gain from their learning experiences. Other names for progress criteria include "learning gain," "improvement scoring," "value-added learning," and "educational growth." Teachers who use progress criteria typically look at how far students have come over a particular period of time, rather than just where they are. As a result, grading criteria may be highly individualized among students.

Types of Learning Criteria Used in Grading and Reporting

- Product criteria
- Process criteria
- Progress criteria

Because of their concerns about student motivation, self-esteem, and the social consequences of giving grades, few teachers use product criteria solely in determining grades. Instead, most routinely base their grading procedures on some combination of these three types of learning criteria (Brookhart, 1993; Frary, Cross, and Weber, 1993). The majority of teachers also vary the criteria they employ from student to student, taking into account individual circumstances (Truog and Friedman, 1996). Although teachers do this in an effort to be fair, the result is a "hodgepodge grade" (Brookhart, 1991) that includes elements of achievement, effort, and improvement. Interpreting the grade or report thus becomes extremely difficult not only for parents, but also for administrators, community members, and even the students themselves (Friedman and Frisbie, 1995). A grade of A, for example, may mean that the student knew what was intended before instruction began (product), didn't learn as well as expected but tried very hard (process), or simply made significant improvement (progress).

Recognizing these difficulties in interpretation, most measurement experts recommend the use of product criteria exclusively in determining students' grades. They point out that the more process and progress criteria come into play, the more subjective and biased grades are likely to be (Ornstein, 1994). How can a teacher know, for example, how difficult a task was for students or how hard they worked to complete it?

Many teachers point out, however, that if product criteria are used exclusively, some high-ability students receive high grades with little effort while the hard work of less talented students is seldom acknowledged. Take, for example, the case of two students enrolled in a physical education class. The first student is a well-coordinated athlete who can perform any task the teacher asks without even putting forth serious effort—and typically does not. The second student is struggling with a weight problem but consistently tries hard, exerts extraordinary effort, and also displays exceptional sportsmanship and cooperation. Nevertheless, this student is unable to perform at the same level as the athlete. Few teachers would consider it fair to use product criteria exclusively in determining these two students' grades.

Teachers also point out that if only product criteria are considered, low-ability students and those who are disadvantaged—students who must work hardest—have the least incentive to do so. These students find the relationship between high effort and low grades unacceptable and, as a result, often express their displeasure with indifference, deception, or disruption (Tomlinson, 1992).

A practical solution to the problem of these diverse learning criteria, and one that increasing numbers of teachers and schools are using, is to establish clear indicators of product, process, and progress criteria and then report each separately (Stiggins, 2001; Wiggins, 1996). In other words, grades or marks for effort, work habits, or learning progress are separated from assessments of achievement and performance. The key to success in doing this, however, rests in the clear specification of those indicators and the criteria to which they relate. This means that teachers must plainly describe the criteria they will use to evaluate students' achievement, effort, and progress, and must openly communicate these criteria to students, parents, and others (Guskey, 1994). Several examples of reporting forms that do this are included in Chapter Four.

Deciding What Sources of Evidence to Use

Still another grading challenge teachers face is determining what sources of evidence they will use in determining students' grades.

Because any single source of information can be flawed and may not accurately represent a student's true achievement or level of performance, it's essential that teachers consider multiple sources of evidence. But whereas most teachers use more than one type of evidence in determining students' grades, they vary widely in the particular evidence they choose and in how they combine or summarize that evidence (McMillan, Workman, and Myran, 1999). Some of the major sources of evidence used by teachers in determining students' marks or grades include the following.

Major Exams or Compositions

Especially in middle schools and high schools, teachers use students' scores on major examinations and on major papers or compositions as an important component in determining grades. While many teachers prepare their own examinations, others use assessments included as supplements to their textbook series. Scores from these examinations or compositions are tallied and weighted in a variety of ways and generally reflect product-grading criteria. If scores from exams or compositions completed early in the marking period are compared to parallel assessments administered at the end of the marking period to determine improvement, however, these would be considered progress criteria.

Class Quizzes

Class quizzes are shorter assessment devices that teachers use on a regular basis to check on students' learning progress. Quizzes are best suited for formative purposes; that is, they help teachers identify students' learning problems and plan subsequent remediation strategies. As such, they represent process-grading criteria. Still, many teachers include the results from class quizzes in determining students' grades.

Reports or Projects

Teachers at all levels have students prepare reports or projects to demonstrate what they have learned. While most reports and projects are individual endeavors, some are designed to involve students in cooperative learning teams. Reports and projects allow students to demonstrate in-depth learning and permit different forms of expression that often cannot be shown in exams or compositions. When accompanied by scoring criteria that articulate the qualities of good work (Andrade, 2000; Arter and McTighe, 2001), reports and projects represent product-grading criteria.

Student Portfolios

Portfolios are collections of students' work. Although typically used to gather examples of students' writing, portfolios can be applied in any subject area. They might include samples of students' mathematics activities, science reports or projects, or social studies papers. Most portfolios are used for summative purposes and represent product-grading criteria. Certain kinds of portfolios are purely formative, however. They are developed to give students opportunities to reflect on their own work and to try to improve it, thereby serving process criteria (Arter and Spandel, 1992). Still others are designed to demonstrate students' progress over time by showing both early and more recent work samples.

Exhibits of Students' Work

Some teachers use exhibits of students' work as a basis for grading. The most common examples include science projects and art or technology exhibits. Although these typically represent product-grading criteria, they can be valuable learning tools that help students identify the qualities of good work and learn to recognize those qualities in their own work. Students also benefit through the process of selecting examples to exhibit, articulating the reasons for their selection, and finally assembling those examples in the exhibit (Brookhart, 1999).

Laboratory Projects

Science and technology teachers frequently build their classes around a series of laboratory experiments or projects that students are expected to complete. When incorporated within instructional activities, these projects allow students to demonstrate more complex levels of learning and offer valuable information on process criteria. Like reports, however, laboratory projects typically are evaluated in terms of specified product-grading criteria.

Notebooks or Journals

Many teachers require their students to keep notebooks or journals as part of a course. Although generally considered an instructional tool used to assist student learning, some teachers evaluate students' notebooks or journals and include these scores or marks as process-grading criteria.

Classroom Observations

Especially in the early elementary grades, many assessments of student learning are based on teachers' classroom observations. When related to specific criteria that are communicated to students during instruction, classroom observations yield product-grading criteria information. Many teachers also use observations to guide what they do instructionally, in which case they reflect process or progress criteria.

Oral Presentations

Students' oral presentations can take many forms. They include assessments of students' answers to the questions raised in class discussions, their explanations of solutions to complex mathematics problems, or their oral responses in a foreign language class. They also include evaluations of oral presentations of projects or reports. Again, when directed toward clear achievement targets and accompanied by specific scoring criteria, oral presentations denote product-grading criteria.

Homework Completion

Many teachers keep track of whether or not students complete their homework assignments and include this as part of the grade. But as we'll see later, the way in which most teachers consider homework doesn't reward students for completing assignments. Rather, it punishes students for not completing them. If homework is assigned to aid students' learning, then it's difficult to justify lowering the grade of otherwise high-performing students for assignments not completed. Similarly, researchers suggest that the missing assignments for poor-performing students may be more a symptom of poor understanding than a cause (Cooper, 2001). Homework completion clearly reflects process-grading criteria.

Homework Quality

Some teachers thoroughly check homework assignments, assess the quality of students' work, and use those assessments in determining students' grades. But like class quizzes, homework is best suited for formative purposes to help identify and then remedy students' learning problems. Like homework completion, assessments of homework quality represent process-grading criteria.

Class Participation

In some classes teachers keep formal records of students' participation in class and consider these participation rates when assigning grades. They might, for example, keep a running tally of the number of times each student contributes to class discussions. Other teachers use class participation in less formal ways, usually to give a break to those students whose other achievement or performance results might be just below a certain grade cut-score (Truog and Friedman, 1996). Class participation is another clear example of process-grading criteria.

Work Habits and Neatness

Some teachers give students special credit if their work is exceptionally neat and well organized, and penalize other students for work that appears sloppy or careless. Although it's certainly possible to develop specific performance criteria for work habits and neatness, this is rarely done. Hence, such assessments typically represent highly subjective judgments by the teacher. Work habits and neatness also represent process-grading criteria.

Effort

To enhance motivation and recognize students' hard work, many teachers include assessments of effort in determining students' grades. In some cases, teachers consider effort to be an expression of students' attitude toward learning or their work ethic. Because explicit criteria for evaluating effort are rarely identified, however, these assessments also tend to be highly subjective judgments on the part of the teacher. Evidence indicates, too, that teachers generally use effort to give a break to only those students who would otherwise receive a low grade, such as a D or F (Truog and Friedman, 1996). Effort is another example of process-grading criteria.

Attendance

Recognizing that class attendance is usually highly related to students' academic achievement and performance, some teachers include students' class attendance in their grading procedures. Other teachers consider attendance important because students learn from each other during class sessions and they want to draw attention to these important interactions. In some cases students receive credit for attending class regularly, but more often they are penalized for being tardy or missing class completely. Attendance also reflects process-grading criteria.

Punctuality of Assignments

In an effort to encourage responsible behavior on the part of students, many teachers consider punctuality of assignments in grading. Typically the scores of students who turn in assignments late are lowered, regardless of the quality of that work or the level of performance it reflects. Punctuality is another example of process-grading criteria.

Class Behavior or Attitude

As described in Chapter Two, students' behavior and the attitudes they display in class sometimes influence teachers' judgments in determining grades. Some teachers include specific behavior indicators among their grading criteria, such as "Remains attentive during class sessions," or "Shows appropriate respect for the teacher and other class members." More often, however, behavior and attitude assessments tend to be ill defined and inconsistently applied. Behavior and attitudes generally represent process-grading criteria.

Progress Made

Many teachers consider the improvements students have made in their performance over a particular period of time when determining grades. Assessing progress generally requires multiple measures that can be used to demonstrate what has been gained or the degree of improvement. It also requires specification of clear indicators of progress. In all cases, however, these are indicators of progress-grading criteria.

Typical Sources of Grading and Reporting Evidence

Major exams or compositions	Homework completion
Class quizzes	Homework quality
Reports or projects	Class participation
Student portfolios	Work habits and neatness
Exhibits of students' work	Effort
Laboratory projects	Attendance
Notebooks or journals	Punctuality of assignments
Classroom observations	Class behavior or attitude
Oral presentations	Progress made

Relating Evidence to Purpose

When asked to indicate which and how many of these sources of evidence they use in grading and reporting student learning, teachers tend to vary greatly. Some base grades on as few as two or three of these indicators, while others include evidence from as many as fifteen or sixteen. This is true even among teachers from the same school.

The reason for this tremendous variation among teachers appears to be the lack of clarity regarding the purpose of grading and reporting. When the purpose is unclear, decisions about the most appropriate evidence are extremely difficult to make. Because the appropriateness of each of these sources of evidence varies depending on the identified purpose, decisions about purpose must always be made first.

If, for example, the expressed purpose of the grades or marks included in a reporting form is to communicate students' current level of achievement or performance, then the evidence used should represent an accurate picture of what they know and are able to do. Sources of evidence that clearly reflect how they got there or process-grading criteria—such as homework, class participation, and effort—should not be included in determining that grade.

This doesn't mean, of course, that process-grading criteria cannot or should not be reported. These are important criteria that have a clear place in reporting procedures. It implies only that these criteria must be reported *separately* and not included as part of a grade or mark that's to represent students' current achievement or performance level. Serious interpretation problems come about mostly when these different types of evidence are combined in a single grade or mark.

To accomplish an array of reporting purposes requires the use of multiple reporting methods and multiple grades or marks. In later chapters we will explore how reporting results separately from various sources of evidence greatly facilitates the communication process and can enhance both teaching and learning (see Brookhart, 1999). The biggest challenge is developing the good judgment and the written, oral, and interpersonal communication skills such comprehensive reporting systems require.

Summary

Grading and reporting present teachers with many difficult challenges, including (1) limiting the negative aspects of subjectivity, (2) balancing instructional concerns with grading requirements, (3) establishing grading criteria, (4) deciding what sources of evidence to use, and (5) relating that evidence to their purpose in grading. Although it's likely that teachers will always struggle with these challenges, a better understanding of their consequences and various strategies to address them will lead to better grading practices and policies.

4

· ·

Grading and Reporting Methods

Simple measures of student learning have little meaning in themselves. Knowing that a student got a score of 60 on a particular exam, for example, tells us nothing about the quality of that performance. This measure gains meaning only when it's compared to something else. If we knew, for example, that a score of 60 translates to a letter grade of B, to a level 3 performance on a four-point achievement scale, or to a "Proficient" but not "Exceptional" performance rating, then we would know more precisely just what that number meant. These bases of comparison are examples of grading methods. They provide information about the quality of that performance as judged by the teacher or another competent person.

Teachers use a variety of different grading methods in reporting the results of their evaluations of students' achievement or performance. In this chapter we'll focus on six of the most common methods:

- Letter grades
- Plus and minus letter grades
- Categorical grades
- Percentage grades
- Standards-based grading
- Narratives and comments

We will describe each method, how it's typically applied, its major advantages and principal shortcomings, and how it can be used most effectively. We'll also explore some of the common fallacies and misunderstandings regarding each of these methods. Although there are other methods of grading, most are adaptations of these six major types.

The goal of this chapter is to help you become more knowledgeable about these different grading methods so that you can better interpret what they mean. While no grading method is appropriate under all conditions, a better understanding of these methods is sure to result in more effective communication between educators and parents.

Letter Grades

Letter grades are undoubtedly the most common and best known of all grading methods. In most instances letter grades compose a five-level grading scale, labeled by the first five letters of the alphabet. The grade of A represents the highest level of performance, B the next level, then C, D, and finally E or F for the lowest level.

Letter grades have been used in schools since the early part of the twentieth century and remain the most prevalent grading method in high schools, colleges, and universities. Teachers at these levels assign letter grades to all forms of students' work, including quizzes, compositions, projects, experiments, and even homework assignments. Many also use letter grades for summary evaluations of students' achievement or performance over a six- or nine-week marking period, semester, or entire academic year. Reporting forms that use letter grades typically record a single grade for each subject or course, similar to the one shown in Exhibit 4.1.

In some reporting forms, one set of letter grades is used to summarize students' performance in academic subject areas such as language arts, math, science, and social studies, while another set is used to report evaluations of their work in art, music, and physical

Exhibit 4.1. Typical Letter Grade Reporting Form.

Subject	Marking Period				
	1	2	3	4	Final
Language arts	B	A			
Mathematics	C	C			
Science	B	B			
Social studies	C	B			
Health	A	A			

education. The grade categories for these latter subject areas are usually limited to three levels. For example, E, S, and N might be used to designate "Excellent," "Satisfactory," and "Needs Improvement." Reporting forms that require teachers to judge students' learning skills, work habits, or class behavior commonly use only three letter grades as well.

Letter Grade Descriptors

Despite their simplicity, the true meaning of letter grades isn't always clear. What teachers wish to communicate and what parents interpret the grade to mean often are not the same (Waltman and Frisbie, 1994). To clarify the meaning of letter grades, therefore, most schools include a key or legend on the reporting form that pairs each letter grade with a word or descriptive phrase. These descriptors are provided to ensure more accurate interpretations of the grades or marks. If not carefully chosen, however, descriptors can lead to additional complications and misunderstanding.

In one particular school, for example, the reporting policy states, "Report card grades reflect students' progress on grade-level learning goals." In other words, the grades are supposed to describe how students are doing in terms of learning criteria that have been established for that grade level. But the words used to describe each letter grade in the legend on the report card include the following:

Key (Less Desirable)

A = Outstanding

B = Above average

C = Average

D = Below average

F = Failing

At least three of these five descriptors (Above Average, Average, and Below Average) reflect norm-referenced comparisons rather than criterion-referenced standards. That is, they compare a student's progress to that of other students, not to specific learning goals. Most parents rightly interpret "average" to mean "in the middle of the group." However, this tells us nothing about "students' progress on grade-level learning goals." An "average" grade of C might be pretty good if most of the other students are making excellent progress. But it might be quite dismal if the majority of students are struggling.

In this example the descriptors don't match the stated intent of the reporting form. If letter grades truly represent progress on "grade-level learning goals," then more appropriate descriptors might be

---

Key (More Appropriate)

A = Excellent

B = Good

C = Satisfactory

D = Poor

F = Unacceptable

These descriptors communicate teachers' criterion-related evaluations of students' achievement or level of performance. They help parents make sense of the grade and understand more fully the teacher's summary judgments. They also avoid the negative effects often associated with norm-referenced comparisons.

Advantages and Shortcomings

Letter grades offer a brief description of students' achievement and level of performance, along with some idea of the adequacy of that performance (Payne, 1974). Because most parents experienced letter grades during their school years, they also have a general sense of what letter grades mean. For this reason, parents often prefer letter grades to newer, less traditional reporting methods (Libit, 1999).

Despite their simplicity, however, letter grades also have their shortcomings. First and probably most important, their use requires the combination of lots of different forms of evidence into a single symbol (Stiggins, 2001). As described in Chapter Three, many teachers combine product, process, and progress evidence in a single grade. This makes the grade a confusing hodgepodge that's impossible to interpret, rather than a meaningful summary of students' achievement and performance (Brookhart, 1991; Cross and Frary, 1996).

Second, despite educators' best efforts, many parents interpret letter grades in strictly norm-referenced terms. Probably because the letter grades they received as students reflected their standing in comparison to classmates, parents frequently assume the same is true for their children. To them, a C doesn't represent achievement at the third level of a five-level performance scale, similar to a middle-level belt in a karate class. Instead, a C means "average" or "in the middle of the class."

A third shortcoming of letter grades is that the cutoffs between grade categories are always arbitrary and difficult to justify. If the teacher decides that the scores for a grade of B will range from 80 to 89, for example, the student with a score of 80 receives the same grade as the student with a score of 89, even though there is a nine-point difference in their scores. But the student with a score of 79—a one-point difference—receives a grade of C. Why? Because the teacher set the cutoff for a B grade at 80. Although cutoffs between grade categories are absolutely necessary in any multilevel grading method, where they are set is always arbitrary.

Finally, letter grades lack the richness of other, more detailed reporting methods, such as standards-based grading or narratives. Although they offer a brief description of the adequacy of students' achievement and performance, letter grades provide no information that can be used to identify students' unique accomplishments, their particular learning strengths, or their specific areas of weaknesses.

Recommendation

Because of their long history and general acceptance among high school and college teachers, letter grades probably will continue to be one of the most popular grading methods. But as stressed in Chapter Three, letter grades should always be based on clearly stated learning criteria, not on norm-referenced criteria. In addition, educators should communicate these criteria to students, parents, and other interested persons.

Furthermore, to avoid the dilemma of having to integrate so much information into a single symbol, teachers at all levels should consider using multiple grades to represent their evaluations of different aspects of students' achievement or performance. An example of such a reporting form is shown in Exhibit 4.2. In forms like this one, teachers record separate grades for different aspects of students' achievement within each subject area. In language arts, for instance, teachers might record different grades for reading, writing, speaking, and listening. They might also record separate grades for product, process, and progress criteria.

Using multiple grades relieves teachers of the difficult task of having to combine so many diverse sources of evidence into a single

Exhibit 4.2. Reporting Form with Multiple Grades for Each Subject Area.

	Marking Period				
Subject	1	2	3	4	Final
Language arts					
Reading	B	A			
Writing	B	A			
Speaking	C	B			
Listening	A	A			
Work habits					
Homework	S	E			
Effort	S	E			
Progress	E	E			
Mathematics					
Computations	C	B			
Problem solving	C	B			
Geometric principles	B	B			
Graphic representations	B	A			
Work habits					
Homework	N	S			
Effort	N	S			
Progress	N	E			

symbol. It also provides more detailed information to parents and to students about their achievement and performance. Although this makes the reporting form somewhat more complicated, it allows teachers to communicate more meaningful information by separating product or achievement evidence from that which reflects process and progress criteria. It also offers parents information that is both diagnostic and prescriptive.

Plus and Minus Letter Grades

To provide more precise descriptions of students' levels of achievement or performance, some educators add a plus (+) or a minus (–) to letter grades. This allows a single grade category to be divided into three levels. The B category, for example, is divided among B+ designating the high level, B for the middle level, and B– for the low level. Most schools that use plus and minus grades keep the A as the highest grade, although some include an A+. Most also maintain only one failing grade of F.

Like many grading issues, the appropriateness of plus and minus grades is hotly debated. Advocates stress that the wide variation in achievement among students in a single grade category demands finer discrimination (Abou-Sayf, 1996). They insist there are real differences between a "high B" and a "low B," and that plus and minus grades allow them to communicate these obvious differences. Furthermore, some survey data indicate that parents favor the use of plus and minus grades on report cards (Schulz, 1999). Opponents counter that the criteria by which these distinctions are made are typically so fuzzy that such fine discrimination is inherently invalid (see Dwyer, 1996). They point out that without clearly defined learning standards and well-refined assessments based on those standards, such minute distinctions are dubious at best. It's like using a razor to cut pudding.

Advantages and Shortcomings

The seriousness of arguments over plus and minus grades contrasts sharply with the simplicity of the issue involved. Basically, the issue comes down to whether it's better to have a five-category grade system (A, B, C, D, and F), or a twelve-category grade system (A, A–, B+, B, B–, C+, C, C–, D+, D, D–, and F). But if more categories are better, one might ask, "Why stop at twelve?" There's nothing sacred or particularly special about using twelve categories. Instead, we might consider a scale similar to the one used to express grade-point average: 0.0 to 4.0. If we limited ourselves to only one decimal point, that would yield forty-one grade categories (see Farley, 1995). Or we might move to percentage grades, a method discussed later in this chapter, which yields 101 categories. Increasing the number of grade categories, however, does not come without costs.

Research on rating scales shows that increasing the number of rating categories from four to just six generally lowers both the reliability and validity of the measures (Chang, 1993, 1994). Other studies indicate that scales of five to possibly nine categories are about as many as any qualified judge can reliably distinguish (Hargis, 1990, p. 14). Moreover, as the number of potential grades or grade categories increases, especially beyond five or six, the reliability of grade assignments decreases. This means that the chance of two, equally competent judges looking at the same collection of evidence and coming up with exactly the same grade is drastically reduced. In addition, as the number of grade categories increases, the potential influence of subjective elements becomes greater. In other words, the subtle influence that subjective elements exert on teachers' judgments is more likely to show up when they are required to identify such fine differences in student performance.

Hence, the added precision of plus and minus grades is far more imaginary than real, especially when the criteria are not well defined or clearly spelled out. Even when they are, the use of plus and minus grades requires the identification of eleven cutoffs between twelve distinct grade categories—an ominous challenge for even the most skilled teacher. For these reasons, it's difficult to recommend the use of plus and minus grades at any level of education.

Furthermore, parents' preferences for plus and minus grades tend to be an expression of their desire for more detailed information. There are far better ways to provide this information, however, than by adding more categories to the grading system. As described earlier, teachers might give multiple grades on different components

of the course, different subtopics of study, or different aspects of performance. They could, for instance, give different grades for
achievement, for process elements like work habits and participation in class, and for progress made during the marking period. Instead of giving a single grade for physical education, a teacher might
assign separate grades for concepts, skills, effort, and improvement.

If the reporting form doesn't permit multiple grades, teachers
could supplement the form with a more detailed description of the
learning standards set for the course and each student's progress with
regard to those standards. Such information helps parents understand that the grades stand for something concise, credible, and
honest.

Recommendation

Pluses and minuses really don't add to the precision of grades, nor
do they improve reliability. In the absence of clear performance criteria, adding more categories to the grading system can actually diminish the reliability of grades. A far better way to communicate
students' level of achievement or performance is to limit the number of grade categories to four or five, but offer separate grades on
different components of the course or different aspects of students'
performance. Providing a supplemental narrative description or
component checklist can further add to the communicative value
of the grade. When policies dictate that only a single grade be reported, the performance criteria used to determine the grade should
be spelled out in detail and clearly communicated to students and
parents from the outset of any course of study.

Categorical Grades

In recent years some educators have argued that letter grades label
students and damage their sense of self-esteem, especially those students whose achievement or performance is assigned a low grade.
Others suggest that the negative connotations of low letter grades

stigmatize students and destroy their motivation to learn (Willis, 1993). For these and other reasons, numerous schools have abandoned the use of letter grades altogether, especially at the lower elementary levels (Guskey, 1993). In their place they use categorical grading methods with category labels they believe to be more affirming.

In Kentucky, for example, many elementary schools discontinued the use of letter grades in reporting forms after passage of the Kentucky Education Reform Act and adopted the same category labels used in the statewide assessment system: "Novice," "Apprentice," "Proficient," and "Distinguished" (see Table 4.1). In Nebraska, a similar four-category system is used with the labels "Beginning," "Progressing," "Proficient," and "Advanced." The *Terra Nova* testing program of CTB/McGraw-Hill reports students' scores in five performance levels labeled "Starting Out," "Progressing," "Nearing Proficiency," "Proficient," and "Advanced." Some systems use terms such as "Preemergent," "Emerging," "Developing," "Acquiring," and "Extending" to describe student performance, but such labels are unnecessarily convoluted and often make little sense to parents. Still other schools substitute more neutral symbols for letter grades. For example, the use of ✔–, ✔, ✔+ is quite popular in elementary-level reporting forms, as are numerals such as 1, 2, 3, or 4.

Table 4.1. Examples of Categorical Grading Labels

Kentucky	Nebraska	*Terra Nova*	Other (Less Desirable)
Distinguished	Advanced	Advanced	Extending
Proficient	Proficient	Proficient	Acquiring
Apprentice	Progressing	Nearing Proficiency	Developing
Novice	Beginning	Progressing	Emerging
		Starting Out	Preemergent

....

Advantages and Shortcomings

Categorical grades composed of verbal labels are generally more descriptive than letter grades. Verbal category labels also eliminate the need for a key or legend explaining what each grade category means. This is not the case, however, with categorical methods that use symbols such as check marks or numerals, which still require verbal descriptors to clarify their meaning.

Whether categorical grades are more affirming and have fewer negative connotations than letter grades remains uncertain. Results from our surveys and informal interviews with parents indicate, however, that many parents simply translate these category labels to letter grades they understand. In other words, to them "Advanced" is an A, "Proficient" is a B, and so on. Students may do the same, especially those who have had prior experience with letter grades. So while educators might believe these more affirming category labels soften the blow of being assigned to a low-level category, the message they communicate to parents and students may be little different from what was conveyed by the assignment of a letter grade.

Categorical Grading

An old joke tells of the child who brings home a paper from school with the grade "Super" written across the top. The parents, of course, are well pleased and praise the child mightily.

Then one parent asks, "Is 'Super' the best you can get?"

"Oh, no," proclaims the child. "'Outstanding,' 'Extraordinary,' and 'Stupendous' are all better. 'Super' is just OK."

If parents' interpretation of a grade is not the same as what educators are trying to convey, then better ways of communicating that information must be found.

Categorical grading methods also have many of the same draw-backs as letter grades. When a single grade is assigned to students' achievement or performance in a subject area or course, a great deal of information must be combined into that single categorical label. In addition, parents frequently interpret categorical grades in norm-referenced terms, and the cutoffs between the various categories are often quite arbitrary. Like letter grades, categorical grades also lack the richness of other, more detailed reporting methods, such as standards-based or narrative grading. So although categorical grading methods provide a brief description of the adequacy of students' achievement and performance, they don't offer the kind of information that can be used to diagnose students' learning errors or prescribe remediation strategies.

Recommendation

Although research verifying that more affirming grade category labels reduce the stigma attached to low grades is scant, this seems quite probable. Certainly the connotation of "Novice" or "Beginning" is far less negative that that of "Failing." Furthermore, the use of "failing" grades at the lower elementary level is indefensible under any conditions. Lots of evidence shows that assigning a failing grade to any student's work at this level does more harm than good (see Guskey, 1996). Teachers at these early grade levels would be well advised to eliminate the use of failing letter grades altogether and, instead, use more affirming, verbal grade category labels such as those described above.

Even in more advanced grade levels, it's better to assign a grade of I or "Incomplete" to students' work and expect additional effort, than to assign a letter grade of F. As we will describe later, assigning I grades requires additional resources and specific support mechanisms, along with cooperation from parents. Nevertheless, such a policy can have a very positive impact on student learning and can be highly cost-effective in the long run (Edward Bernetich, personal communication, February 6, 1998).

Percentage Grades

Percentage grades are the ultimate multicategory grading method. Ranging from 0 to 100, percentage grades offer 101 grade categories. Some schools and school districts use percentage grades alone to express teachers' summary judgments of students' achievement or performance in a particular subject area or course. In most schools, however, percentage grades are paired with letter grades by using a common translation table like the one shown below:

Grading Scale

90–100 percent = A

80–89 percent = B

70–79 percent = C

60–69 percent = D

< 59 percent = F

Percentage grades are generally more popular among middle school and high school teachers than they are among elementary teachers. Like letter grades, they have a long history of use in schools and are second only to letter grades in their prevalence on reporting forms.

Advantages and Shortcomings

By including so many grade-level categories, percentage grades allow for maximum discrimination in evaluations of students' achievement and performance. Even when the percentages are translated to letter grades, teachers can still distinguish between a "high B," a "solid B," and a "low B." The use of percentage grades also maximizes the variation among students, making it easier to choose students for individual honors or determine which students should be assigned to special programs. Therefore, if selection and classification are the major purpose of grading, percentage grades are an excellent choice.

Similar to the other grading methods presented previously, however, percentage grades require the blending of lots of different types of evidence into a single grade. This requirement, in turn, makes accurate interpretation of the grade extremely difficult. The increased number of grade categories means an increased number of arbitrary cutoffs between those categories. In other words, the cutoffs are no less arbitrary; there are just a lot more of them. Furthermore, the large number of grade categories and the fine discrimination between them allow for the greater influence of subjectivity in determining the grade. Therefore, as was true with plus and minus grades, the increased precision of percentage grades is far more imaginary than real.

Recommendation

Counter to what many believe, the increased number of grade categories provided by percentage grades does not improve precision, objectivity, or reliability. In fact, in the absence of clearly established performance criteria, the large number of ill-defined categories included in percentage grades actually serves to diminish all these qualities. Especially when reporting policies require that only a single grade be assigned, these negative attributes make percentage grades difficult to justify.

By limiting the number of grade categories to four or five, and offering separate grades for different aspects of students' performance, educators can provide better and far more useful information. Providing a supplemental narrative description or standards checklist describing the learning criteria used to determine the grade for each aspect of the subject further enhances the value of this information. Simply adding more categories to the grading scale cannot satisfy parents' requests for more and better information. Instead, what must be considered are the quality of the information offered and its usefulness to parents, students, and other interested persons.

Standards-Based Grading

In an effort to bring greater clarity to the grading process, many schools have initiated standards-based grading procedures and reporting forms. In most cases this involves a four-step process. First, teams of educators identify the major learning goals or standards that students are expected to achieve at each grade level or in each course of study. Second, performance indicators of those learning goals or standards are established. In other words, educators decide what evidence best illustrates students' attainment of each goal or standard. Third, graduated levels of quality for assessing students' performance are determined. This involves the identification of incremental levels of attainment, sometimes referred to as *benchmarks*, that can be noted as students make progress toward achieving the learning goals or standards (see Andrade, 2000; Wiggins and McTighe, 1998). Finally, educators develop reporting tools that communicate teachers' judgments of students' learning progress and culminating achievement in relation to the learning goals or standards.

Steps in Developing Standards-Based Grading

1. Identify the major learning goals or standards that students will be expected to achieve at each grade level or in each course of study.
2. Establish performance indicators for the learning goals or standards.
3. Determine graduated levels of quality (benchmarks) for assessing each goal or standard.
4. Develop reporting tools that communicate teachers' judgments of students' learning progress and culminating achievement in relation to the learning goals or standards.

Interpreting Standards

Many parents' initial response to a standards-based reporting form is one of uncertainty. After looking over the form, many turn to the teacher and ask, "This is great, but how's my child doing, *really?*" Others inquire, "How is my child doing compared to the other children in the class?" They ask these questions because they're unsure about how to interpret the information in the reporting form and what that information means. Furthermore, when they were in school their teachers used comparative, norm-based reporting systems instead of criterion- or standards-based systems. As a result, they're more familiar with reports that compare students to their classmates rather than with those that compare students' progress to established learning standards and performance criteria.

What parents generally want is a way to make sense of the information included in the reporting form. Their fear is that their child will reach the end of the school year and won't have made sufficient progress to be promoted to the next grade. To ensure this doesn't happen, parents want accurate information that helps them judge the adequacy of their child's progress, and they want that information as early as possible.

To remedy this problem and ensure more accurate interpretations, several schools have begun to use a two-part marking system with their standards-based reporting form. Every marking period each student receives two marks for each standard. The first mark indicates the student's level of progress with regard to the standard. That mark might be a 1, 2, 3, or 4, indicating "Beginning," "Progressing," "Proficient," or "Exceptional." The second mark indicates the relation of that level of progress to established expectations for student learning at this point in the school year. For example, a double-plus (++) might indicate "Advanced for grade-level expectations," a plus (+) might indicate "On target" or "Meeting grade-level expectations," and a minus (–) would indicate "Below grade-level expectations" or "Needs improvement." An example of such a reporting form is shown in Exhibit 4.3, which is adapted from one used in the Bellevue School District in Bellevue, Washington.

The advantage of this two-part marking system is that it helps parents make sense of the information included in the reporting form each marking period. It also helps alleviate their concerns about what they may perceive as low grades and lets them know whether their child is progressing at a rate considered appropriate for the grade level. In addition, it helps parents take a standards-based perspective in viewing their child's progress. Their question is no longer, "Where is my child in comparison to his or her classmates?" but rather, "Where is my child in relation to the learning goals and expectations set for this level?"

It may be, for example, that all students in the class are doing exceptionally well and progressing at a rate considered "Advanced" in terms of grade-level expectations. This would not be possible, of course, in a norm-referenced system, where even those students who are "Advanced" in relation to their classmates might be doing poorly in relation to grade-level expectations. Schools and school districts that use the two-part marking system generally find that parents like the additional information and believe it adds to the communicative value of reporting forms.

Performance-Level Descriptors

As was true with letter grades, standards-based grades that use numerical grading scales also require a key or legend that explains the meaning of each numeral. These descriptors are typically words or phrases that help parents and others understand what each numeral means.

A common set of descriptors used in standards-based reporting forms matches performance levels 1, 2, 3, and 4 with the achievement labels "Beginning," "Progressing," "Proficient," and "Exceptional." If the standards reflect behavioral aspects of students' performance, then descriptors such as "Seldom," "Sometimes," "Usually," and "Consistently" or "Independently" are more common (see Table 4.2).

Exhibit 4.3. Example of a Double-Mark, Standards-Based Reporting Form.

Elementary Progress Report

Student: *T. Nedutsa*		Grade: *1*
Teacher: *Ms. Rotnem*	School: *Bloom Elementary*	Year:

This report is based on grade-level standards established for each subject area.
The ratings indicate your student's progress in relation to the year-end standard.

Evaluation Marks

4 = Exceptional
3 = Meets Standard
2 = Approaches Standard
1 = Beginning Standard
N = Not Applicable

Level Expectation Marks

+ + = Advanced
+ = On Level
− = Below Level

Social Learning Skills and Effort Marks

E = Exceptional
S = Satisfactory
U = Unsatisfactory

READING	1st	2nd	3rd	4th
Understands and uses different skills and strategies to read	1+	2++		
Understands the meaning of what is read	1++	2+		
Reads different materials for a variety of purposes	1+	2−		

Exhibit 4.3. Example of a Double-Mark, Standards-Based Reporting Form, cont'd.

	1st	2nd	3rd	4th
READING cont'd.				
Reading level	1++	2++		
Work habits	S	S		
WRITING	1st	2nd	3rd	4th
Writes clearly and effectively	1++	2++		
Understands and uses the steps in the writing process	1++	2++		
Writes in a variety of forms for different audiences and purposes	1+	2–		
Analyzes and evaluates the effectiveness of written work	N	1+		
Understands and uses the conventions of writing: punctuation, capitalization, spelling, and legibility	1–	2–		
Work habits	S	S		
COMMUNICATION	1st	2nd	3rd	4th
Uses listening and observational skills to gain understanding	1+	2–		
Communicates ideas clearly and effectively (formal communication)	1–	2+		
Uses communication strategies and skills to work effectively with others (informal communication)	N	1+		
Work habits	U	S		

Table 4.2. Examples of Performance Level Descriptors

Performance Level	Achievement Descriptors	Behavioral Descriptors
4	Exceptional	Consistently, Independently
3	Proficient	Usually
2	Progressing	Sometimes
1	Beginning	Seldom

Many reporting forms include a fifth level of "Not Applicable" or "Not Evaluated" to designate standards that have not yet been addressed or were not assessed during that particular marking period. Including such a mark is preferable to leaving the marking space blank, which parents often interpret as something that was missed or neglected by the teacher.

Advantages and Shortcomings

When clear learning goals or standards are established, standards-based grading offers important information about students' achievement and performance to parents, students, and others. If that information is sufficiently detailed, it can be useful for both diagnostic and prescriptive purposes. For these reasons, standards-based grading facilitates teaching and learning processes better than any other grading method.

At the same time, standards-based grading also has its shortcomings. First and perhaps most significant, standards-based grading takes a lot of work. As described earlier, not only must educators identify the learning goals or standards on which grades will be based, they also must decide what evidence best illustrates students' attainment of each goal or standard, identify graduated levels of quality for assessing students' performance, and develop reporting tools that communicate teachers' judgments of students' learning progress. These tasks can add considerably to the workload of teachers and school leaders.

Another shortcoming of standards-based grading is that the reporting forms educators develop are sometimes too complicated for parents to understand. In their efforts to provide parents with "rich" information, educators can go overboard and describe learning goals in unnecessary detail. As a result, reporting forms become cumbersome to handle, time-consuming for teachers to complete, and difficult for parents to interpret.

A third shortcoming of standards-based grading is that it may not communicate the appropriateness of students' progress. Simply reporting a student's level of proficiency with regard to a particular standard communicates nothing about the adequacy of that level of achievement or performance. To make sense of the information included in a standards-based reporting form, parents need to know how that level of achievement or performance compares to the learning expectations that have been established for that particular grade level.

Finally, though standards-based grading can be used at any grade level and in any course of study, most current applications are restricted to the elementary level, where there is little curriculum differentiation. In the middle grades and at the secondary level, students usually pursue more diverse courses of study. Because of these curricular differences, standards-based reporting forms at the middle and secondary levels must vary from student to student. In other words, the marks included on the form would need to relate to each student's achievement and performance in his or her particular courses or academic program. Although advances in technology allow educators to provide such individualized reports, few middle and secondary schools have taken up the challenge.

Recommendation

The grades in standards-based reporting forms provide clear information about each student's learning progress in relation to specific learning goals or standards. Although such forms are typically more detailed and more complex than forms that record letter grades or percentages, most parents value the richness of the information provided, especially if it's expressed in terms they understand and can use. Reporting forms that employ a two-part marking system show particular promise. As described earlier, the first mark describes each student's level of progress with regard to the standard, while the second mark indicates the relation of that level of progress to established grade-level expectations. Although such a system further complicates the reporting form and requires additional explanation, it offers parents important information that can be used to facilitate students' learning.

Successfully implementing standards-based grading and reporting demands a close working relationship among teachers, parents, and school and district leaders. To accurately interpret the reporting form, parents need to know precisely what the standards mean. Well-organized meetings with parents to explain the standards and how to appropriately interpret the reporting forms are essential in gaining parents' acceptance and support.

Narratives and Comments

Narratives are written descriptions of student achievement and performance prepared by the teacher. They represent the oldest of all grading methods. Narratives can be very general or highly specific, depending on the reporting policies of the school and the inclination of individual teachers. Although most common at the elementary level, increasing numbers of middle and high schools have begun to incorporate some form of narrative grading in their reporting forms. Few schools, however, use narrative grading alone. Most combine narrative reports with other grading methods such as letter grades or standards-based grading, and offer the narrative as a way to clarify meaning or present additional explanation.

Reporting forms based on narrative grading are usually quite simple in structure. Most consist of a series of boxes in which teachers record their descriptive evaluations of what students have accomplished and what areas need improvement. Early forms required teachers to write their comments on the reporting form by hand and were extremely time-consuming to prepare. An example of such a form is shown in Exhibit 4.4. In most schools today, however, student records are kept on computer files and the recording process is much easier. Teachers simply access each student's record and then type in the comments they want to have printed on the reporting form.

Narrative grading is most effective when teachers' comments relate to clearly defined learning goals. In particular, comments should focus on students' strengths and what they've achieved during that marking period. When necessary, comments might also offer suggestions as to how any weaknesses might be remedied. Such comments are particularly helpful to parents who want guidance from teachers on how they can best help their child with school work.

Standardized Comment Menus

To simplify narrative grading, many schools have adopted computerized grading programs that allow teachers to select comments from a standardized comment menu (Friedman and Frisbie, 1995). To use such programs, teachers simply scan down a list of standard comments, click on the one or two they want to include, and the computer then prints those comments on the reporting form. While most programs print the entire comment, some print only a comment number and then refer parents to a separate, numbered comment list.

Standardized comment menus represent the briefest form of narrative grading and are always used in conjunction with other grading methods such as letter grades or standards-based grading. Menus typically include both positive and negative comments that cover a wide range of achievement and nonachievement aspects of students' performance (see Exhibit 4.5).

Evidence gathered from parents and teachers shows that both believe it's important to provide more than just grades on reporting forms. Nevertheless, only a small portion of parents and teachers

Exhibit 4.4. Traditional Narrative Reporting Form.

York School District Elementary Reporting Form

Student: R. Samoht	Grade: 2
Teacher: Mr. Yeksug	Year:
School: Tyler Elementary	

Reading

In reading our class has been working on perspective in works of fiction. Although Rachel contributes regularly to class discussions, her reading speed is slow and her comprehension skills need improvement. She could benefit from additional supervised reading time at home.

Writing

This marking period we concentrated on sentence structure in writing. Rachel can construct complex sentences that show deep understanding and creative expression. Her writing has shown significant improvement in recent weeks.

Mathematics

This marking period we worked on basic addition and subtraction skills, along with problem solving. Rachel can solve double-digit addition and subtraction problems, and does exceptionally well with verbal problems applying these skills.

Science

In science we are currently investigating classification systems. Rachel works well with her classmates in cooperative assignments and did a great job on her independent class project.

Exhibit 4.5. Examples of Standardized Computer Comments.

Type of Comment	Example
Positive academic	"Asks appropriate questions"
Positive behavioral	"Behaves appropriately in class"
Negative academic	"Does not understand the subject"
Negative behavioral	"Disturbs other students"
General	"Fails to bring instruments or materials"

Source: Adapted from S. J. Friedman, G. A. Valde, and B. J. Obermeyer, "Computerized Report Card Comment Menus: Teacher Use and Teacher/Parent Perceptions." *Michigan Principal,* 1998, 84(3), 11–14, 21.

think that menu-based comments are adequate (Friedman, Valde, and Obermeyer, 1998). Parents generally want specific, individualized comments and often regard menu-based comments as too impersonal and imprecise.

Results from our surveys and interviews with parents reveal much the same. Few parents indicated that standardized, menu-based comments were helpful and none found them prescriptive. Many parents actually described such comments as "highly impersonal" and illustrated their point by citing how different teachers, teaching different subject areas, often offered the same, word-for-word comment about their child. Listing only a comment number and then referring parents to a standard comment list was identified as the most impersonal of all. Hence, while teachers frequently want to give, and parents frequently want to receive, more information than grades alone provide, neither group found standardized comment menu systems sufficient for this purpose.

Advantages and Shortcomings

Of all grading methods, narratives have the potential to be the most specific and most personalized. Especially if teachers' comments are based on specific learning goals that students and parents understand, narratives can offer a clear description of achievement, performance, and learning progress. When used in conjunction with other grading methods such as letter grades or categorical grades, narratives bring added clarity and richness to the information included in the reporting form. Some research indicates, in fact, that many parents like narrative reports for these very reasons. They are more personal, less competitive, and convey more explicit information about students' learning progress (Hall, 1990).

At the same time, narrative grading also has its shortcomings. Among all grading methods, narratives show the greatest variation among teachers. Some teachers offer detailed descriptions; others include only a brief statement or two. Good narratives are also extremely time-consuming to prepare, even with the help of computerized grading programs.

Perhaps the greatest drawback of narratives, however, is that they frequently do not communicate the adequacy of students' performance (Afflerbach and Sammons, 1991). Even parents who recognize the limitations of letter grades and other categorical grading methods often prefer these methods to narrative reports because they consider them more accurate and more precise (Allison and Friedman, 1995).

Recommendation

The flexibility, versatility, and richness of the information that narratives can offer make them an important component in any grading and reporting system. Although many parents consider narrative grading alone to be insufficient, most welcome narrative comments as a supplement to other grading methods and believe they bring added precision to the grading process. Narratives give teachers the opportunity to clarify the marks or grades they record. Furthermore, by focusing their comments on specific learning goals, teachers can prescribe solutions to identified learning problems and can offer ideas on how parents could become more involved in their child's education at home.

To emphasize parents' roles as partners in the learning process, many narrative reporting forms include a section for the parents to complete. In other words, instead of just signing the reporting form and returning it to school, parents are asked to add their comments or reactions in this section. They might, for example, pose questions, comment on their child's progress, or request a conference. This helps facilitate two-way communication between home and school, and gives parents the opportunity to become more involved in their child's school work.

Summary

Grading methods communicate teachers' judgments of students' achievement and performance. In the process of grading, teachers convert different types of descriptive information and various measures of students' performance into grades or marks that summarize their evaluations of students' accomplishments. Grades provide parents, students, and others with the means to interpret the teacher's professional judgments. When grades are referenced to specific criteria or learning standards, they identify students' specific strengths as well as areas where improvement is needed.

Letter grades, categorical grades, and percentage grades all offer brief descriptions of the adequacy of students' academic performance. If only a single grade is reported for each subject or course, however, many different sources of evidence must be combined into that single symbol or category label. This makes the grade a hodgepodge of information that is impossible to interpret. One way to remedy this problem is to use multiple grades, each one representing a different aspect of the subject or course, or a different dimension of students' performance. Standards-based grading and narratives allow teachers to describe in more detail the performance criteria or learning standards used to determine students' grades. Although these methods require additional work on the part of educators, they also give grades clearer meaning and more practical significance.

In essence, grading is much more a challenge in effective communication than simply a process of quantifying students' achievement. What matters most in grading is not what method is used or what symbols are employed, but what message is communicated. When the message teachers want to communicate is accurately interpreted by parents, students, and others, grading has served its communication purposes well.

5

Special Issues in Grading and Reporting

Though grading and reporting will always be debated, today we have lots of evidence on what practices benefit students and encourage learning and what practices don't. In some areas this evidence is highly consistent and offers clear prescriptions for improvement.

In this chapter we'll focus on several of the most controversial grading issues. These include grading "on the curve," selecting valedictorians, setting grade cutoffs, using weighted grades, and dealing with grade inflation. We'll consider what we know about each of these issues and explore prescriptions for better practice. Hopefully, these discussions will lead to improvements that benefit students and satisfy both parents and educators.

Grading on the Curve

As described in Chapter Three, some teachers use the normal probability curve as a basis for assigning grades (see box on page 73). They rank order students in terms of some combination of indicators and then assign grades based on set percentages of students to receive each grade. For example, the top 10 to 20 percent might receive A's, the next 20 to 30 percent B's, and so on. This practice yields highly consistent grade distributions from one teacher to the next. In other words, every class receives the same percentage of A's, B's, C's, and so forth. But the consequences of this practice are overwhelmingly negative. Strong evidence shows that it's detrimental to the relationships among students and to the relationships between teachers and students (Krumboltz and Yeh, 1996).

Grading on the curve makes learning a highly competitive activity in which students compete against one another for the few scarce rewards (high grades) distributed by the teacher. Under these conditions, students readily see that helping others threatens their own chances for success (Gray, 1993; Johnson, Johnson, and Tauer, 1979; Johnson, Skon, and Johnson, 1980). High grades are not attained through excellence in performance, but rather by doing better than one's classmates. As a result, learning becomes a game of winners and losers, and because the number of rewards is kept arbitrarily small, most students are forced to be losers (Haladyna, 1999; Johnson and Johnson, 1989).

Most parents can recall negative experiences shared in classes where they were graded on the curve. Many remember the anger they felt toward a high scoring student who "inflated the curve" and, in their minds, caused other class members to receive a low grade. Others remember being the object of their classmates' anger because they were that high-scoring student. Stories also abound of students hiding books in the library so that their classmates couldn't use them or removing equipment needed in projects or experiments in order to enhance their chance for a high grade. Consequences such as these deny students the opportunity to work together and help each other attain valuable, shared learning goals.

Perhaps most important, grading "on the curve" communicates nothing about what students have learned or are able to do. Rather, it tells only a student's relative standing among classmates based on what are often ill-defined criteria. Students who receive high grades might actually have performed very poorly, but simply less poorly than their classmates. In addition to promoting unhealthy compe-

---

On Grading on the Curve

John Bishop of Cornell University recently related an interesting story about education in Ireland that is relevant here. In Ireland there are national educational standards against which all students are evaluated. Ireland considered changing this policy and leaving evaluation criteria to local educational units and teachers. When teachers were polled to assess their reaction, they opposed the change. Why? Because they felt the proposed change would pit them against their students and their students against one another. When there is a common standard, it is the goal of every teacher to have all students achieve that standard, and it is a common goal of all students to help their classmates make the grade. The competition is against the standard, not against one another.

Contrast this with our system, in which any teacher who dared to give the whole class grades of A because all students had reached mastery would at best be criticized for lacking standards and contributing to grade inflation. Contrast this with our system, in which the principal of an affluent suburban Philadelphia high school recently remarked that group learning activities were difficult to arrange in his school because students could not get beyond worrying about how they were to be graded in comparison to others in their group. The idea that they could all excel together was alien to them (Gray, 1993, p. 374).

---

tition, grading on the curve destroys perseverance and other motivational traits, and is generally unfair to students (Haladyna, 1999).

Recommendation

In any educational setting where the central purpose is to enhance student learning, grading and reporting should always be done in

reference to specific learning criteria, rather than in reference to
normative criteria. Because normative criteria or "grading on the
curve" tell nothing about what students have learned or are able to
do, they provide an inadequate description of student learning. At
all levels of education, teachers should identify what they want their
students to learn, what evidence best verifies that learning, and
what criteria are most appropriate in judging that evidence. Grades
based on specified learning criteria have direct meaning and are far
better communication tools.

Selecting Valedictorians

Although most teachers today understand the negative consequences of grading on the curve and have abandoned the practice,
many fail to recognize other common school practices that yield
similar negative consequences. One of the most prevalent is the way
schools select class valedictorians. There's nothing wrong, of course,
with recognizing excellence in academic performance. But in selecting the class valedictorian, most schools operate under the traditional premise that there can be *only one*. This often leads to
severe and sometimes bitter competition among high-achieving students to be that "one." Early in their high school careers top students figure out the selection procedures and then, often with the
help of their parents, find ingenious ways to improve their standing
in comparison to classmates. Again, to gain that honor a student
must not simply excel; he or she must outdo the other students in
the class. And sometimes the difference among these top students
is as little as one-thousandth of a decimal point in a weighted grade-
point average.

An increasing number of high schools have resolved this problem by naming multiple valedictorians. This is similar to what colleges and universities do in naming graduates *magna cum laude* and
summa cum laude. West Springfield High School in Fairfax County,

Virginia, for example, typically graduates fifteen to twenty-five vale-dictorians each year (David Smith, personal communication, July 2, 1999). Every one of these students has an exemplary academic record that includes earning the highest grade possible in numer-ous honors and Advanced Placement classes. Instead of trying to distinguish among these exceptional students, the faculty at West Springfield High School decided that all should be named valedic-torians. In other words, rather than creating additional, arbitrary criteria in order to discriminate among these top students (consid-ering, for example, their academic record from middle school or even elementary school), they decided to recognize the excellent achievement and performance of the entire group. And because the faculty at West Springfield High School believes their purpose as teachers is not to *select* talent, but rather to *develop* talent, they take great pride in these results. All the valedictorians are named at the graduation ceremony, and one student, selected by his or her fellow valedictorians, makes a major presentation.

Some might object to a policy that allows multiple valedictori-ans, arguing that colleges and universities demand such selection and often grant special scholarships to students who attain that sin-gular distinction. But current evidence indicates this is rarely the case. In processing admission applications and making decisions about scholarships, college and universities are far more interested in the rigor of the curriculum students have experienced (Bracey, 1999). In fact, an index composed of the number of Advanced Placement courses taken, the highest level of math studied, and total number of courses completed has been shown to be a much stronger predictor of college success than standardized test scores, grade point average, or class rank (Adelman, 1999). The rigor of the academic program experienced by the valedictorians from West Springfield High School has helped them gain admission and win scholarships to many of the most selective colleges and universities in the nation.

Recommendation

The process by which class valedictorians are selected is another example of a practice that is continued, not because of its merits, but simply because "we've always done it that way." Better understanding of the consequences of such practices allows us to implement improved and more appropriate policies (see Guskey, 2000). Recognizing excellence in academic performance is a vital aspect in any learning community. But such recognition need not be based on arbitrary standards and detrimental competition. Instead, it can and should be based on clear models of excellence that exemplify our highest standards and goals for students. And if many students meet these high standards of excellence, all the better.

Setting Grade Cutoffs

Another widely debated grading issue is how to set appropriate cutoffs between grade categories. This seems particularly important in translating percentages to letter grades. In some schools, for instance, the cutoff for the grade of A is set at 90 percent, for the B at 80 percent, and so on. While many educators find this reasonable, others contend that "higher" standards should be required. In their classes, therefore, they might set the cutoff for the grade of A at 92 percent or even 95 percent, believing that by increasing the cutoff by these additional percentage points they have raised both the standards and the expectations for students' performance.

On the surface such arguments seem reasonable. And, indeed, raising the cutoff percentage set for each grade category may increase the challenge for students to some degree. A far more important consideration, however, is the difficulty of the tasks students are asked to perform or the complexity of the assessment questions they're required to answer. The cutoff percentage representing an excellent level of performance on an extremely challenging task or very difficult set of questions might be quite different from what would be considered excellent on a relatively simple task (see Guskey, 2001).

Suppose, for example, a teacher wanted to assess students' basic knowledge of United States presidents. To do so, the teacher might use an "open-ended" question, also known as a "short-answer" or "completion" question, such as

---

1. Who was the seventeenth president of the United States?

For most students, this is an extremely difficult question that fewer than 10 percent are able to answer correctly. Its high level of difficulty is actually rather odd because most people know that Abraham Lincoln was the sixteenth president and they also know that the name of the president who succeeded Lincoln had the same name as the president who succeeded John Kennedy: Johnson. Putting these two pieces of information together, however, is quite difficult for the majority.

So the teacher might consider asking the same question in a different format, this time as a multiple-choice question. For example:

---

2. Who was the seventeenth president of the United States?
    A. Abraham Lincoln
    B. Andrew Johnson
    C. Ulysses S. Grant
    D. Millard Fillmore

This remains a fairly difficult question for most students. Because of the multiple-choice format, however, about 30 percent are able to answer correctly. Of course, if all students simply chose an answer at random, the multiple-choice format would allow 25 percent to select the correct response.

Suppose the teacher next adjusted the possible responses, making the distinctions a bit more obvious:

3. Who was the seventeenth president of the United States?
   A. George Washington
   B. Andrew Johnson
   C. Jimmy Carter
   D. Bill Clinton

Now identifying the correct response is much easier, and about 60 percent of students are able to answer correctly. The teacher could probably assume that those students who are still unable to identify the correct response have very limited knowledge of United States' presidents.

Of course, the teacher could make a final adjustment to the possible responses in order to make the question easier still:

4. Who was the seventeenth president of the United States?
   A. The War of 1812
   B. Andrew Johnson
   C. The Louisiana Purchase
   D. A Crazy Day for Sally

About 90 percent of students are able to answer this question correctly. Those who don't are usually drawn to the response "A Crazy Day for Sally" because they recognize it as the one response that doesn't belong with the others.

Some might argue that knowing who was the seventeenth president of the United States is a rather trivial learning outcome—and that might be true. The point is that while each of these questions assesses the same learning objective, same goal, or same achievement target, each varies greatly in its difficulty.

Suppose that questions similar to each of these four types were combined in a larger assessment designed to measure students' learning in an instructional unit. Those four assessments would present vastly different challenges to students, and the scores students attained on such assessments undoubtedly would reflect those differences. Would it be fair to set the same grade percentage cutoffs for each of those four assessments?

The Challenge of Cutoffs

Focusing on only a percentage cutoff is seductive but very misleading because tests and assessments vary widely in how they're designed. Some assessments include questions that are so challenging that students who answer a low percentage correctly still do very well.

Take the Graduate Record Examinations (GRE), for example, a series of tests used to determine admission to graduate schools. Individuals who answer only 50 percent of the questions correctly on the GRE Physics test perform better than more than 70 percent of those who take the test. For the GRE Mathematics test, 50 percent correct would outperform approximately 60 percent of the individuals who take the test. And among those who take the GRE Literature test, only about half get 50 percent correct (Gitomer and Pearlman, 1999).

In most classrooms, of course, students who answer only 50 percent correctly would receive a failing grade. Should we conclude from this information that prospective graduate students in physics, mathematics, and literature are a bunch of "failures"? Of course not. Percentage cutoffs without careful examination of the questions or tasks students are asked to address are just not that meaningful.

Researchers suggest that an appropriate approach to setting cut-offs must combine teachers' judgments of the importance of concepts addressed and consideration of the cognitive processing skills required by the questions or tasks (Nitko and Niemierko, 1993). Using this type of grade assignment procedure shifts teachers' thinking so that grades on classroom assessments and other demonstrations of learning reflect the quality of student thinking instead of simply the number of points students attain. It incorporates the value the teacher places on successful performance and the teacher's perception of the level of thinking that students must use to answer a question or perform a task.

Making matters even more complicated is that the challenge or difficulty of an assessment task is also directly related to the quality of the teaching. Students who are taught well and provided ample opportunities to practice and demonstrate what they have learned are likely to find well-aligned performance tasks or assessment questions much easier than students who are taught poorly and given few practice opportunities. Hence, a 90 percent cutoff might be relatively easy to meet for students who are taught well, while a 70 percent cutoff might prove exceptionally difficult for students who experience poor-quality teaching.

Recommendation

Setting grade cutoffs is a vital and necessary part of nearly all grading and reporting procedures. But setting cutoffs is a more complex process than most educators and parents think. In most cases it's also much more arbitrary than most imagine.

We must keep in mind that mathematical precision in setting cutoffs is not a substitute for sound professional judgment. Raising standards or increasing expectations for students' learning cannot be accomplished simply by raising the cutoff percentages for different grades. Instead, it requires thoughtful examination of the tasks students are asked to complete and the questions they are asked to answer in order to demonstrate their learning. It also requires consideration of the quality of the teaching students experienced prior to the assessment.

Using Weighted Grades

A common practice in many high schools today is to assign more weight or credit to the grades earned in courses considered exceptionally challenging than is assigned to regular or general courses (Mitchell, 1994). Honors courses and those designed to prepare students for Advanced Placement (AP) examinations, for example, might be given a weight of five credits, while regular or general courses would have a weight of four credits. Other schools simply adjust grading scales so that a B in an honors or AP course is considered equivalent to an A in a regular or general course. Some schools make further adjustments by assigning less weight or credit to lower-level courses or remedial courses.

The use of weighted grades is typically justified on the grounds of fairness. They are seen as a way to compensate or reward those students who enroll in more challenging courses. Many educators also believe that weighted grades are an enticement to bright students who might choose a less rigorous program of studies unless some form of special recognition is offered.

Before opting to use weighted grades, however, two important questions need to be addressed: What is their purpose? and How will they be used? In most schools today, weighted grades are used to differentiate students' performance for the purpose of selection. In determining who will be named on the honor roll, for instance, weighted grades allow students enrolled in challenging courses with lower grades to be eligible, while ensuring the exclusion of students with high grades in only remedial courses. Weighted grades are also a major factor in many high schools when it comes to naming a valedictorian. Apart from these selection and differentiation functions, however, weighted grades have little utility. No research evidence shows that they motivate students to enroll in more challenging courses or deter students from enrolling in lower-level or remedial courses (see Gilman and Swan, 1989).

Recommendation

As stressed earlier, students who attain high levels of achievement or performance deserve special recognition. Likewise, students should be encouraged to enroll in challenging academic programs and those who do well should be appropriately distinguished. Honor roll membership and other forms of academic recognition (letters, special commendations, and so on) serve this purpose well.

At the same time, however, educators must be clear about the criteria used in conferring such distinctions. Specifically, they must decide whether the high standards associated with such "honors" mean that the courses are challenging in the absolute sense of specific knowledge and skills or simply challenging for that particular student. If the former, then weighted grades will allow more students in challenging courses to be recognized, while making students with disabilities who receive A's and B's in lower-level courses ineligible. If the latter, then weighted grades are irrelevant and unnecessary. In either case, however, it is an issue of differentiation and selection—not an academic issue.

The use of weighted grades in selecting the valedictorian is another matter altogether. Recall our discussion earlier in this chapter of the dilemmas caused when selection is restricted to a single student. The recommendation there was to name multiple valedictorians or to follow a process similar to that used in colleges and universities where graduates are distinguished as *magna cum laude* and *summa cum laude*. This provides special recognition for those students who have distinguished themselves academically, while eliminating the detrimental effects that result from the competition among students for that singular distinction.

Some argue that weighted grades help college officials distinguish honors or AP courses in students' transcripts (Lockhart, 1990; Talley and Mohr, 1991), and this may be true. But there are other, equally precise and efficient means of identification. For example, such courses can be specially marked, numbered differently, or highlighted in the transcript. Aside from this labeling function, weighted grades have little relevance.

In essence, the issue of weighted grades comes down to the basic purpose of grading and reporting. If the purpose is to communicate teachers' judgments about students' achievement and performance to parents, the students themselves, or others, then it's difficult to justify the use of weighted grades. On the other hand, if the purpose of grading is to select, identify, or group students for certain educational paths, programs, or honors, then weighted grades take on considerable significance. Remember, however, that no single grading method or reporting tool can serve both these purposes well. Once decisions about purpose are made, questions about weighted grades will be clearer and much easier to address.

Dealing with Grade Inflation

Another hotly debated grading issue is grade inflation. Critics of education frequently argue that more students today receive high grades, not because of excellence in achievement or performance, but because of new grading schemes and teachers' concerns about students' self-esteem. According to these critics, teachers have relaxed their standards and, as a result, grades have become meaningless (Beaver, 1997). To counter this problem teachers are encouraged to "hold down" grades and restrict the number of high grades they assign (Agnew, 1993). Those opposed to such measures are labeled as apathetic to the problem of grade inflation (Hills, 1991) and unwilling to take steps necessary to curb this dilemma (Gose, 1997; Zirkel, 1995).

Careful research on grade inflation shows, however, that the problem may be more imagined than real. At the college level, for example, studies show that although students' grade point averages (GPAs) have generally risen over the last two decades, this increase is largely the result of changes in the characteristics of entering students (Kwon and Kendig, 1997). Especially at selective colleges and universities, entering students today are older and more talented than those who entered a decade ago. Furthermore, in recent years most colleges and universities have launched major efforts to improve the instructional skills of their faculty. With more talented students and better teaching, wouldn't an increase in students' GPAs be expected?

Another recent study investigated the issue of grade inflation at the high school level by comparing students' high school GPAs with their scores on the Scholastic Assessment Test (SAT) (Bracey, 1998). If grade inflation were occurring, then we would expect over time that the SAT scores of students with the top GPAs would be declining. In other words, if teachers are really assigning A's to undeserving students, then the average SAT scores of A students should go down.

This study found the opposite trend, however. Both the math and verbal scores of the top 20 percent of students have risen in recent years, indicating that top ranked students are actually accomplishing more during their high school careers. The study's author points out that SAT scores are never a particularly good measure of educational trends because students who take the SAT are self-selected and the size and demographics of this group of students change over time. Still, these data offered no support for the idea that grade inflation is prevalent in high schools or that students' high grades are undeserved.

Recommendation

The problem of grade inflation is not simply that more students are receiving high grades. Rather, the problem rests in the meaning of the grades assigned. When grades reflect teachers' judgments of students' achievement and performance in reference to clearly defined learning goals or standards, the meaning of those grades is clear. When challenged about the grades they assign or accused of grade inflation, teachers only need point to the goals or standards used in determining the grades. So long as those standards are sufficiently rigorous and appropriate for that grade level or course, the assigned marks or grades can be easily defended. The best way to fight grade inflation, therefore, is not to assign fewer high grades but to push for clearer standards.

Remember, however, that developing more stringent guidelines for grading is not the same as raising learning standards (see Agnew, 1995). Many popular assumptions about how to address the question of standards (raising cut-scores, weighting grades, freeing teachers from external pressure, and so on) emphasize grades rather than standards (Basinger, 1997). In essence, they focus on the yardstick rather than on what it measures. Once learning goals and standards are clearly defined, the problem of grade inflation pretty much disappears.

Grade Inflation Is Not the Real Issue

Grade inflation deeply concerns many school officials today and leads to many heated debates. Unfortunately, most of these debates focus on the wrong issues and, as a result, the solutions proposed are misguided. The problem with grade inflation isn't simply that more students are receiving high grades. Rather, it is that we're not sure what those grades mean.

The question that needs to be addressed in these debates is "What is the purpose of grading?" If, as some teachers believe, the purpose of grading is to discriminate among students, then we must maximize the differences between students in terms of their performance. Since it's difficult to distinguish among students if many do well, we need to make sure the differences in their performance are as large as possible.

Of course, nothing maximizes those differences better than poor teaching. When students are taught poorly, only those who are able to teach themselves learn well and receive high marks. The majority of students who need the help and assistance of their teachers learn very little and receive the low marks.

Maximizing differences among students is typically accompanied by "grading on the curve." This means that students are graded according to their relative standing among classmates. Grading on the curve makes it easy to adjust for grade differences between classes by simply requiring that only a small percentage of students, say the top 20 percent, receive the highest grade.

But when students are graded on the curve, a high mark doesn't represent excellent performance, as some might think. It means only that the performance was somewhat better than that of others in the class, all of whom might have performed miserably.

Grading on the curve also makes learning highly competitive. Students must compete among themselves for the few scarce rewards (high grades) distributed by the teacher. Under these conditions students avoid helping each other because doing so is detrimental to their chances for success. Getting a high grade doesn't mean performing excellently. It means doing better than your classmates.

On the other hand, if the purpose of grading is to reflect how well students have learned, then we must follow different procedures. First we must clarify what we want students to learn and be able to do. Second we must identify clear criteria or standards by which their learning will be judged. That means we must decide in advance what evidence best represents what students have learned.

Teaching then becomes an organized and purposeful effort to help all students meet those standards. The goal is to develop talent, not simply to identify and select it.

Grades that reflect well-defined learning standards have direct meaning. They describe what students have accomplished and the skills they've acquired. Grades based on learning standards also bring new significance to discussions of differences in grade distributions across classes.

Students' grades in some teachers' classes might be higher because the standards are less rigorous. A comparison of related learning criteria would address this issue. It also might be, however, that some teachers are simply better than others at helping their students attain rigorous and challenging learning standards. Such evidence would be invaluable in efforts to improve instructional quality.

The problem is that defining clear learning standards and deciding what evidence best reflects those standards is hard work. It takes lots of time, clear thinking, and dedicated effort. Teachers don't always agree on what standards are appropriate or what evidence should be used to verify students' attainment of those standards. But isn't this precisely the kind of debate that should be going on in schools today?

Until we precisely identify what students are expected to learn, articulate the criteria by which their learning will be judged, and clearly communicate these criteria to students, grading will remain an arbitrary and highly subjective process that victimizes more students than it helps. (Adapted from an editorial by Guskey, 1999.)

Summary

Modern research evidence offers important insights into several hotly debated issues regarding grading and reporting. This same evidence also provides direction to efforts to develop more effective practices and policies.

We know, for example, that grades should always be based on clearly defined learning criteria and never "on the curve." Basing grades on normative criteria or students' relative standing among classmates makes learning a highly competitive endeavor for students. It also diminishes motivation, damages relationships among students, and diminishes the relationship between teachers and students. The process of selecting valedictorians similarly can lead to deleterious competition among students if schools restrict selection to a single student. Recognizing multiple valedictorians, similar to what colleges and universities do in naming graduates *magna cum laude* and *summa cum laude*, acknowledges excellence in academic performance without the negative consequences.

Setting grade cutoffs is a more complex process than most teachers and parents imagine. It requires thoughtful examination of the procedures used to assess student learning, as well as consideration of the quality of teaching students experience. The issue of weighted grades, on the other hand, comes down to basic questions about purpose. If the purpose of grading is to select, identify, or group students for certain programs or honors, then weighted grades have great value. But if the purpose of grading is to communicate teachers' judgments about students' achievement and performance, then weighted grades have little significance.

Grade inflation occurs when high grades are assigned for substandard levels of achievement or performance. The best way to address concerns about grade inflation, therefore, is not to simply restrict the number of high grades that can be assigned. Rather it is to clarify the goals or standards used in determining the grades. So long as those standards are appropriate and sufficiently rigorous, the assigned marks or grades have direct meaning and can be easily justified.

6

. . . .

Developing Better Grading
and Reporting Systems

In this chapter we turn to building a comprehensive reporting system. Because it's impossible to serve all reporting needs with a single instrument, parents and educators must work together to develop reporting systems that include a variety of communication tools. Such systems typically begin with a report card, but then add other reporting tools to meet different reporting purposes and needs. I will describe some of these tools and explain how each can be used. I'll also show how adhering to principles of honesty and fairness can unite parents and educators in their efforts to build an efficient and effective reporting system.

The Importance of Purpose

The most important consideration when selecting the tools to include in a reporting system is each tool's purpose. This requires thinking about three vital aspects of communication:

1. What information do we want to communicate?
2. Who is the primary audience for that information?
3. How will that information be used?

Once the purpose is clear, it's a lot easier to select the reporting tool that best serves that particular purpose.

Many school communities make the mistake of choosing reporting tools first, without giving careful attention to the purpose. In numerous schools, for example, educators charge headlong into the development of a standards-based report card without first addressing core questions about why they're doing it. Their efforts usually encounter unexpected resistance and rarely bring positive results. Both parents and teachers see the change as a newfangled fad that presents no real advantage over more traditional reporting methods. As a result, most of these efforts end up being short-lived experiments that are abandoned after a few troubled years of implementation.

Efforts that begin by clarifying purposes, however, make intentions clear from the start. This clarity not only helps mobilize everyone involved in the reporting process, it also keeps efforts on track. The famous adage that guides architecture also applies to reporting student learning: *Form follows function*. In other words, purpose must always come first. Once the purpose or function is decided, questions about form become much easier to address.

The Challenge of Effective Communication

Parents and teachers alike know the formidable barriers to increasing parent involvement in school activities. Some of the most pressing challenges include both parents working, single parents with heavy responsibilities, transportation difficulties, child-care needs, cultural and language barriers, and some parents just too stressed or too depressed to care (Kirschenbaum, 1999). Yet research shows that most parents are willing to take the steps necessary to help their children succeed in school. What they need, however, is specific guidance from the school, and especially their child's teacher, on how best to offer that help (Chrispeels, Fernandez, and Preston, 1991).

Effective communication between school and home requires the provision of high-quality information. Parents want to know, on a regular basis, how their child is doing in school. But they also want that information in a form they understand. Many parents see the report card as the primary source of such information. That's why most parents indicate they would like to receive report cards more often. A reporting *system* that includes multiple reporting tools can offer high-quality information at different times throughout the school year and address this major parental concern.

Tools for a Comprehensive Reporting System

Most schools' reporting systems include a variety of reporting tools. In fact, advances in communication technology make the number and variety of options available virtually unlimited. The most highly regarded reporting systems typically include a mix of traditional and modern reporting tools. Some of those most commonly used are listed in the box below and described in the following pages.

Tools That Might Be Included in a
Comprehensive Reporting System

Report cards	Personal letters
Notes attached to report cards	Evaluated projects or assignments
Standardized assessment reports	Portfolios or exhibits of students' work
Phone calls	Homework assignments
Weekly or monthly progress reports	Homework hot lines
School open houses	School Web pages
Newsletters	Parent-teacher conferences
	Student-teacher conferences
	Student-led conferences

Report Cards

Report cards are the centerpiece in nearly every school's reporting system. If its primary purpose is to communicate information to parents about teachers' judgments of students' achievement and performance, then parents should be closely involved in developing the report card. To serve as an effective communication tool, parents have to understand the information included in the report card (Wiggins, 1994, 1997). They also must be able to interpret that information correctly and use it appropriately to guide any improvements that might be necessary.

But if the primary purpose of the report card is to communicate information to students for self-evaluation, then it's students who must be able to understand and accurately interpret the information included. This, in turn, means that students should be involved in the development of the report card so that their perspectives and concerns can be taken into account.

Whatever purpose is chosen, however, that purpose should be clearly stated on the report card itself. It should be printed in a box on the top of the report card or on the first page. Clearly stating the purpose helps everyone know what the report card represents, the intended audience, and how the included information should be used.

Notes Attached to Report Cards

One way many principals and teachers strengthen their relationships with students and parents is to attach short, personal notes to each student's report card. In some cases the notes are intended for the parents. More often, however, they address the students themselves (see Exhibit 6.1).

These notes have a twofold purpose. First, they express the principal's or teacher's interest in each student's learning progress. Second, they allow principals and teachers to recognize students' accomplishments and to encourage improvement efforts.

Exhibit 6.1. Example of a Report Card Note from the Principal or Teacher

> *Great job in math, Chris!.*
> *Next time, let's try to bring up those marks in social studies, too!*

In our interviews with parents and students, we were surprised to find how much they value and appreciate these small notes. Many indicated that it's the first thing they read on the report card and that these notes are always saved. Although preparing such notes requires time and commitment on the part of principals and teachers, they're an effective communication tool that reinforces positive home-school relations (Giba, 1999).

Standardized Assessment Reports

Many schools and school districts administer commercially prepared, standardized tests and assessments to gain another perspective on students' achievement and performance. These assessments are typically given just once a year, and because they must be sent to the testing company to be scored, results generally are not available to teachers, students, or their parents until several months later.

Students' scores on standardized assessments are usually compared to score distributions obtained from a "national sample" of students who are of similar age or at the same grade level. Results are then reported in norm-referenced scales such as percentiles, grade equivalents, or some other standard score. Test manufacturers prepare score summaries for each student, along with brief descriptions of what the scores mean. These summaries are kept in students' permanent school files and also sent home to parents, who do their best to make sense of the results (see McMillan, 2001).

Of all reporting tools, standardized assessment reports are probably the most frequently misinterpreted. The complex statistical procedures used to generate students' scores commonly mystify parents and educators alike. Two students, for instance, could answer the same number of questions correctly and yet have very different scores because of differences in the difficulty of the questions they answered. The student who answered several difficult questions correctly but missed several easy questions would receive a higher score than a student who answered correctly only the easy questions. Even seemingly simple scores such as "grade equivalents" are usually misunderstood (Hills, 1983).

Complicating matters further is that most standardized assessments are not well aligned with the curriculum being taught and, hence, tend to be an inadequate measure of how well students have learned (Barton, 1999). In addition, correct interpretations of results typically require extensive training for both parents and educators.

Phone Calls

Phone calls are one of the easiest and most efficient means of communication between parents and educators. Of all reporting tools, however, phone calls are probably the most underutilized and misused.

In our surveys, for example, we discovered that over 70 percent of parents indicated they "feared" phone calls from school. When we asked them to explain, many told us that in their experience, teachers called home for only one of two reasons. The first reason is that their child has done something wrong and is in trouble. The second reason is that their child is sick or hurt. Is it any wonder that parents fear phone calls from school if these are the only reasons educators call them?

We should add, however, that educators often express similar apprehensions about parents' phone calls. Many indicate that the only time a parent calls is in response to a problem or to register a complaint. Rarely do teachers get phone calls from parents to compliment them on helping their child or in response to some other positive event.

To change these negative perceptions, many schools have initiated programs in which teachers make regular phone calls to parents. When the parent answers the teachers emphasize that they have no set agenda for the call. Instead they simply want to hear any concerns parents might have and answer any questions.

Teachers can use the regular phone calls to inform parents of special events and to invite their participation. This might include classroom celebrations, choir performances, science fairs, or open house meetings. Calls also provide parents with the opportunity to keep teachers informed about events in students' lives that might be affecting their schoolwork. Without them, for example, the teacher might not know that one quiet girl often had late assignments because she was competing in gymnastics, that a boy's father was taking over custody, that several fourth-grade girls were picking on one another at recess, or that a beloved grandfather had died. In addition, phone calls give parents the opportunity to check on the information their children bring home from school (Gustafson, 1998).

Both teachers and parents relate that the first phone call is always the most difficult. Time and again teachers have described parents who answer the phone and, learning the call is from their child's teacher, ask, "What did he do now?" Automatically they assume something must be wrong. Likewise, teachers tend to assume that a call from a parent is the sign of a problem. Although making phone calls to parents takes time and effort on the part of teachers, most indicate that the benefits far outweigh the costs. This is especially true when the parent ends the call with "I'm really glad you called."

Weekly or Monthly Progress Reports

Another reporting tool that many school staffs use to inform parents about what's going on in school and how to become involved is weekly or monthly progress reports. In some cases these are short checklists or mini report cards that give parents a brief summary of students' learning progress. Others simply inform parents about the curriculum and teachers' expectations.

An example of one such report is shown in Exhibit 6.2. Teachers complete this form and hand out copies to students to take home to their parents at the beginning of each month. It informs parents about the curriculum focus of the class and the planned learning goals. Equally important, it offers parents specific suggestions about how they might help at home. Parents deeply appreciate these forms. Plus, they frequently contribute to improvements in student learning.

Exhibit 6.2. Example of a Monthly Class Report.

| **Morton Middle School** |
| **Parent Information and Involvement Form** |
| Teacher _____ Class_____ |
| During the next month, the major topics we will be studying are |
| Our goal in studying these topics is for students to be able to |
| Parents can help at home by |

School Open Houses

A school open house is a brief meeting, usually held in the evening, where parents are invited to the school to visit their child's classrooms and to meet with the teachers. Open houses are frequently parents' first encounter with their child's teachers and the teachers' first opportunity to interact with their students' parents.

Open house meetings rarely involve detailed discussions about individual students. The limited time available simply doesn't allow it. Nevertheless, a school open house is an effective communication tool for parents to use in gathering information about the school and their child's teacher (Langdon, 1999). It provides an opportunity for parents to learn about what the teacher has planned for the class, what learning goals have been set, and how the teacher intends to help students reach those goals. During the meeting parents can also gather information about homework policies, required projects, classroom procedures, and tips on how they can help at home. Although teachers generally convey this information in their presentations during the meeting, parents shouldn't hesitate to raise questions if such issues are not addressed. Questions that relate to their child only, however, should be reserved for a parent-teacher conference that can be scheduled for a later time.

Newsletters

When it comes to fostering communication between school and home, most parents as well as most educators consider conventional forms of communication more effective than newer ones, such as Internet Web sites and hot lines (Landgon, 1999). And among the more conventional forms, newsletters are always rated as one of the most effective.

Newsletters provide parents and others with everyday details about school. They often describe upcoming events, thank parents by name for their assistance, announce student award winners, and provide ideas on specific learning activities parents can do with their children. Some newsletters include profiles of new teachers or staff members, and many include a special column by the principal (Kirschenbaum, 1999). Most schools distribute newsletters once each month and parents typically assist in their preparation.

In addition to regular newsletters, many schools distribute an attractive calendar and handbook to parents at the beginning of each school year. The calendar notes school events, indicates when interim reports and report cards will be distributed, encourages parents' involvement, and offers detailed suggestions on how parents can support their child's education at home (Kirschenbaum, 1999). The handbook offers information about the school and staff members, describes school policies, and indicates where and how parents can find more details.

Personal Letters

Personal letters to parents allow teachers to model honest communication by notifying parents when their child has done exceptionally well or by informing parents as soon as academic or behavioral problems arise. Parents' personal letters to teachers allow them to keep teachers informed of occurrences in students' lives that might affect their school work or their participation in school activities. Such letters can open pathways to further communication and help facilitate cooperation in solving problems (Kreider and Lopez, 1999). The use of electronic letters or e-mail, another excellent communication tool, is discussed later in this chapter.

Evaluated Projects or Assignments

Evaluated projects and assignments represent a highly effective means for teachers to communicate learning goals and expectations to parents. But the form of this evaluation information is vitally important. Projects or assignments that come home with only a single mark or grade at the top of the page provide neither students nor their parents with much useful information. Although they may

communicate the teacher's overall appraisals of students' achievement or performance, they offer no guidance for improvement.

Parents need direction from educators, and particularly their
child's teacher, on how they can help. Evaluated assignments or assessments that include specific comments from the teacher, along
with clear suggestions for improvement, offer parents that needed
direction. Projects or papers accompanied by explicit scoring guides
similarly provide parents with a clear description of what the
teacher expects and the criteria by which students' work is judged.
With this information parents can make sure their efforts at home
are well aligned with what the teacher expects at school. Parents
also shouldn't hesitate to ask teachers for this kind of information
if it's not provided.

Portfolios and Exhibits of Students' Work

Another efficient and highly effective way of sharing information
about students' achievement and performance is through evaluated
samples of students' work included in a portfolio. Portfolios are simply collections of evidence on student learning that serve three
major purposes: (1) to display students' work around a theme, (2)
to illustrate the process of learning, or (3) to show growth or
progress (Davies, 2000). Some portfolios are specific to a class or
subject area, while others combine students' work across several subjects (Robinson, 1998). Most parents are enthusiastic about the use
of portfolios as a reporting tool, and often indicate they learn more
from the portfolio than they do from the report card (Balm, 1995).

Most schools use portfolios in conjunction with report cards to
clarify the marks or grades included in the report card. In some
schools, however, portfolios serve to inform parents on a more regular and ongoing basis. Certain schools, for example, use "Friday
Folders" to keep parents abreast of their children's performance. A
collection of evaluated papers, assignments, and assessments, along
with notes from teachers and notices of school events, are included

in the folder and sent home each Friday. Parents sign the folder each week and record any comments or questions they have. Students then return the folder to their teacher the following Monday.

Exhibits of students' work represent yet another good way to communicate information about their achievements. The athletic and fine arts departments in schools have long scheduled sporting events, concerts, and plays for parents and interested community members to attend. These events communicate important and meaningful information to those who watch or listen about what students can do. Exhibits designed expressly for the purposes of communicating how well students perform in academic tasks can do the same (Brookhart, 1999).

The best portfolios and exhibits are accompanied by clearly stated qualities of good work that help students and their parents recognize these qualities. Teachers also must teach their students how to select the examples to exhibit and how to articulate the reasons for their selections. These are important assessment-related skills that help students become more thoughtful judges of their own work and lead to higher levels of student performance.

Homework Assignments

Most teachers see homework as a way to offer students additional practice on what they learned in class and to extend their involvement in learning activities. Some teachers use homework to give students the opportunity to explore topics of special interest through reports and independent projects. But homework is also an excellent way for teachers to communicate with parents. Through homework assignments parents can learn what the teacher is emphasizing in class, what is expected of students, and how students' work will be evaluated (Cooper, 1989).

Students' engagement in homework is closely related to measures of achievement and academic performance at the high school level, although this relationship has more to do with the quality of homework in which students engage than simply the quantity. At the elementary level, however, the relationship between homework and performance in school is more modest. In elementary grades homework serves best to inform parents of what students are doing in school and to involve parents in students' learning (Cooper, 2001).

Homework assignments at the elementary level, therefore, are often designed so that parents and students can work together. For example, an assignment might involve questions that students are to ask their parent or guardian, issues that students and parents are to explore together, or a procedure for students to complete and then have their parent check. Experiences such as these give parents the opportunity to become involved in their children's schoolwork, encourage good work habits, and emphasize the importance of learning (Cooper, 2001).

Homework Hot Lines

To facilitate completion of homework assignments, many schools develop "homework hot lines." The simplest hot lines permit students and their parents to telephone the school, follow a series of simple instructions, and then hear a recorded message from the teacher describing the homework assignment for that day. Some teachers simply describe the assignment and the due date in their message. Others specify the goal of the assignment, offer suggestions for completion, and outline the criteria by which the assignment will be evaluated. These messages allow students to check on assignments and clarify those of which they're unsure. They also permit students who are absent from school to get a head start on make-up work.

In some schools, homework hot lines are actually staffed by teachers or teaching assistants who offer direct assistance to students on their homework assignments. Students who get stuck on some aspect of an assignment can call the hot line and get immediate help. They need not wait until their next class to ask a question or to get the assistance they need. Although setting up homework hot lines requires additional expense and effort on the part of educators, the service offers a variety of benefits to both students and their parents.

School Web Pages

As schools become increasingly sophisticated in their use of technology, more are establishing their own Internet Web pages. Some school Web pages simply offer information about the school, administrators, and faculty; school policies; and the time and dates of special events. Others include information about various programs of study and each course or class within the program. In addition to a general description of the classes, many include information about the learning standards or goals, the grading criteria or scoring rubrics for particular class projects, and a schedule of assignments. In some cases descriptions are regularly updated to include information about daily homework assignments and special class events.

Another important advantage of school Web pages is that they offer the opportunity for two-way communication. Most Web pages include a list of the e-mail address of each school administrator, teacher, and staff member. Parents who have questions or concerns can correspond with their child's teacher directly and need not worry about interrupting the teacher's busy schedule. Teachers, in turn, can respond to parents' questions and concerns at a time convenient to them. Furthermore, e-mail allows both teachers and parents the time to think about their responses, include pertinent information, offer suggestions or recommendations, and then keep a record of the communication. Although most schools report that relatively few parents correspond with teachers or staff members via e-mail, those who do find it a very useful form of communication.

Parent-Teacher Conferences

Parent-teacher conferences hold special promise as a reporting tool because the communication is interactive and can be highly individualized. Teachers can select different pieces for information or even various themes to discuss for different students (Brookhart, 1999). Conferences also offer teachers and parents the opportunity to discuss a wide range of school-related but nonacademic aspects of learning, such as attendance and tardy rates, class participation, attentiveness, social interactions, and class behavior (Nelson, 2000).

Regardless of their format, however, parent-teacher conferences must be carefully planned. Many of the parents we interviewed, for example, expressed occasional disappointment with parent-teacher conferences. Some said that the time allotted for the conference was too short to get a clear picture of how their child was doing. Others related stories of having to stand in long lines to have only a few minutes with the teacher. Teachers expressed different but equally serious frustrations. Several described spending hours preparing for conferences and then having only a few parents show up. The parents who did show up often were not the ones with whom the teacher really hoped to speak. Other teachers told of the difficulties they encountered in dealing with angry and disgruntled parents.

When well planned, however, parent-teacher conferences can be key to developing a positive working relationship between parents and teachers. The most effective parent-teacher conferences focus on four major issues (Davies, 1996):

1. What is the student able to do?

2. What areas require further attention or skill development?

3. How is the student doing in relation to established learning standards for students in a similar age range or grade level?

4. What help or support does the student need to be successful?

With careful planning and organization, parent-teacher conferences can be both informative and productive. They are an effective way to build positive, collaborative relationships between parents and teachers, and should be part of every school's comprehensive reporting system.

Student-Teacher Conferences

Another highly effective but often neglected conference form is the student-teacher conference. Like parent-teacher conferences, student-teacher conferences require careful planning and organization. In particular, if the conferences are held during class time, teachers must ensure that students not involved in the conference are engaged in meaningful learning activities. Student-teacher conferences also have their own dynamics and require different approaches to communication about academic work. Nevertheless, they provide for both students and teachers a form of one-to-one, interpersonal communication that cannot be achieved through other communication formats.

Some teachers conduct student-teacher conferences just twice per year, while others schedule conferences with students at the beginning of each marking period. This regular schedule of conferences allows them to review students' immediate past work while setting improvement goals for forthcoming marking periods or instructional units.

Student-Led Conferences

Yet another highly effective conference form is student-led conferences. In the typical parent-teacher conference and student-teacher conference, teachers lead the discussion regarding students' learning progress. In contrast, in a student-led conference the students are responsible for leading the discussion and reporting on their learning to parents. The teacher serves primarily as facilitator and observer (see Bailey and Guskey, 2001).

Most teachers organize student-led conferences so that several conferences (typically four) are conducted at the same time in the classroom, with family groups seated far enough apart to allow privacy. The teacher circulates among family groups, stopping long enough to make pertinent comments and answer questions. Students direct the conversation during the conference, focusing on the work samples they have included in their conference portfolio and on their performance in relation to expected learning goals or standards.

The real power in this conference format is that students take responsibility for reporting what they have learned. To prepare for this responsibility, students must be given regular opportunities to evaluate and reflect on the quality of their work. They also must be given guidance in how to organize their work in a portfolio, and how to explain their work to others. In other words, students must be actively involved in all aspects of the reporting process.

Student-led conferences also are an effective means of promoting parent involvement. Schools that have implemented student-led conferences consistently report dramatic increases in parent attendance at conferences (Little and Allan, 1989).

In our surveys and interviews we learned that parents, too, have high regard for student-led conferences. One parent of an elementary student said, "I didn't know my son could speak so well about his work. He usually tells me he 'learned nothing today.' He really does know what he's doing!" Parents of high school students similarly expressed appreciation for all of the preparation and reflection that went into the portfolio of the student's work. Many told us that they especially liked having their son or daughter present to talk about concerns and to answer questions during the conference.

Student-led conferences represent a highly effective way to communicate directly and authentically with parents. When students direct the reporting process, they communicate information in a form everyone can understand and use. As learning becomes increasingly complex from kindergarten throughout high school, the portfolio becomes a more detailed reporting tool that demonstrates students' growth and progress over time. Reviewing the portfolio during the conference becomes a learning experience for everyone involved. As such, student-led conferences are an especially important part of a comprehensive reporting system.

Technology and Grading

Most educators today use technology as an aide in grading and reporting tasks. Computerized grading programs have become increasingly popular in recent years and present educators with a wide range of grading and record-keeping options. Some of these programs simply help teachers keep more detailed records on students' learning progress (Eastwood, 1996). Others are more complex and allow teachers to present evidence on students' achievement and performance in a variety of formats, including computer displays, video report cards, and digital portfolios.

Video Report Cards and Digital Portfolios

One of the most widely used alternative formats for communicating information about students' achievement and performance is the video report card. Video recordings of individual students' performances present a dynamic record of what was learned. Furthermore, by recording students' performance at several times during the school year, teachers can show specific aspects of learning progress (Brewer and Kallick, 1996).

On the elementary level, for instance, many teachers record students reading orally, presenting a mathematics problem, discussing a class project, or performing a physical exercise at the beginning of the marking period and again at the end. This allows students, their parents, and others to see improvements firsthand (Greenwood, 1995). Similarly at the secondary level, video recordings of students' oral presentations, problem explanations, or musical performances provide a permanent record that can be reviewed and re-examined as a tool for further learning (Berg and Smith, 1996).

Some schools formalize the video recording process by having students develop video portfolios of their work. Others with more advanced technology encourage students to develop digital portfolios that include a broad array of work samples and exhibits of their accomplishments. Although video report cards and digital portfolios may not soon replace more standard types of reporting forms, they are a highly effective supplement to such forms and greatly enhance the quality of information provided.

Electronic Gradebooks

Electronic gradebooks have also become increasingly popular in recent years (Huber, 1997). These computer software programs provide data management systems that make it easy for teachers to record and tally large amounts of numerical information (Vockell and Fiore, 1993). They are particularly well suited to the point-based grading systems of middle and high school teachers who often record numerical data on the performance of a hundred or more students each week (Feldman, Kropf, and Alibrand, 1996).

For all their advantages, however, electronic gradebooks also have their shortcomings. Perhaps the most serious is that many educators believe the mathematical precision of computerized grading programs yields greater objectivity in grading. Others believe this increased precision enhances fairness in the grading process. Unfortunately, neither of these beliefs is true.

Computerized grading programs and electronic gradebooks yield neither greater objectivity nor enhanced fairness. At best, they offer teachers a tool for manipulating data. Although these programs may make record keeping easier, they do not lessen the challenge involved in assigning grades that accurately and fairly reflect students' achievement and level of performance.

Consider, for example, the data in Table 6.1. The scores on the left reflect the performance of seven students over five instructional units. The bold-faced scores on the right side of the table represent summary scores for these students calculated by three tallying methods. The first method is the simple arithmetic average of the unit scores, with all units receiving equal weight. The second is the median or middle score from the five units (Wright, 1994). The third method is the arithmetic average, deleting the lowest unit score in the group. This method is based on the assumption that no one, including students, performs at a peak level all the time (Canady and Hotchkiss, 1989). These are the three tallying methods most frequently used by teachers and most commonly included in electronic gradebooks and other computerized grading programs.

Consider, too, the following explanations for these score patterns:

Student 1 struggled in the early part of the marking period but continued to work hard, improved in each unit, and performed excellently in unit 5.

Student 2 began with excellent performance in unit 1 but then lost motivation, declined steadily during the marking period, and received a failing mark for unit 5.

Student 3 performed steadily throughout the marking period, receiving three B's and two C's, all near the B-C cutoff.

Student 4 began the marking period poorly, failing the first two units, but with newfound interest performed excellently in units 3, 4, and 5.

Student 5 began the marking period excellently but then lost interest and failed the last two units.

Student 6 skipped school (an unexcused absence) during the first unit but performed excellently in every other unit.

Table 6.1. Summary Grades Tallied by Three Methods.

Student	Unit 1	Unit 2	Unit 3	Unit 4	Unit 5	Average Score	Grade	Median Score	Grade	Deleting Lowest	Grade
1	59	69	79	89	99	79	C	79	C	84	B
2	99	89	79	69	59	79	C	79	C	84	B
3	77	80	80	78	80	79	C	80	B	79.5	C
4	49	49	98	99	100	79	C	98	A	86.5	B
5	100	99	98	49	49	79	C	98	A	86.5	B
6	0	98	98	99	100	79	C	98	A	98.8	A
7	100	99	98	98	0	79	C	98	A	98.8	A

Grading standards:
90–100 percent = A
80–89 percent = B
70–79 percent = C
60–69 percent = D
59 percent or less = F

Student 7 performed excellently in the first four units but was caught cheating on the assessment for unit 5, resulting in a score of 0 for that unit.

As you can see, while all three of these tallying methods are mathematically precise, each yields a very different pattern of grades for these seven students. If the arithmetic average is used (Method 1), all seven students would receive the same grade of C. If the median is used (Method 2), there would be only two C's, one B, and four A's. And if an arithmetic average is calculated with the lowest score deleted (Method 3), there would be only one C, four B's, and two A's. Note, too, that the one student who would receive a grade of C using Method 3 had unit grades consisting of just two C's and three B's. What is more important, no student would receive the same grade across all three methods. In fact, two students (4 and 5) could receive a grade of A, B, or C, depending on the tallying method employed!

The teacher responsible for assigning grades to the performance of these seven students has to answer a number of difficult questions. For example, which of these three methods is the fairest? Which method provides the most accurate summary of each student's achievement and level of performance? Do all seven students deserve the same grade, as the arithmetic average (Method 1) indicates, or are there defensible reasons to justify different grades for certain students? And if there are reasons to justify different grades, can these reasons be clearly stated? Can they be fairly and equitably applied to the performance of all students? Can these reasons be clearly communicated to students before instruction begins and to parents after the grades go home? Would it be fair to apply them if they were not?

The nature of the assessment information from which these scores are derived could make matters even more tangled. Might it make a difference, for example, if we knew that the content of each unit assessment was cumulative? In other words, the assessment for unit 2 contained material from units 1 and 2, and the unit 5 assessment included material from all five previous units. And if it did, would this make these grading decisions any easier, or would it further complicate summary calculations?

What should be evident in this example is that the use of computerized grading programs will not solve these complex grading problems. Although such programs can simplify numerical record keeping, the mathematical precision they offer doesn't make the grading process any more objective or any fairer. Calculating a summary score to the one hundred thousandth decimal point doesn't yield a more accurate depiction of students' achievement and level of performance. Each teacher still must decide what information goes into the calculation, what weight will be attached to each source of information, and what method will be used to tally and summarize that information.

Above all, we have to recognize that teachers' professional judgments will always be an essential part of the grading process. Teachers at all levels must make carefully reasoned decisions about the purpose of the grade, the components that will be included in determining the grade, how those components will be combined and summarized, and what format will be used in reporting those summaries. While computerized grading programs and electronic gradebooks are useful tools that help teachers record and mathematically tally numerical data, they do not relieve teachers of the professional responsibilities involved in making these crucial decisions. In the end, teachers must still decide what grade offers the most accurate and fairest description of each student's achievement and level of performance over a particular period.

Summary

The diverse reporting needs present in schools today cannot be satisfied with a single instrument, such as a report card. Instead, parents and educators must work together to develop reporting systems that include a variety of communication tools. A well-designed report card will be the centerpiece of such a system. But it also will include an assortment of reporting devices, each with a specific communication purpose and designed to meet a particular communication need. Reporting systems based on the principles of honesty and fairness serve to unite parents and educators in their efforts to help students learn.

Technology presents educators with countless options when it comes to communicating information about students' achievement and performance. Video report cards and digital portfolios offer parents authentic information about what students know and are able to do. Computerized grading programs and electronic gradebooks greatly simplify record-keeping tasks by allowing teachers to gather increased amounts of evidence and then tally that evidence in highly efficient ways. At the same time, however, technology does not alleviate the need for sound and intelligent professional judgment in the grading process. It also doesn't alleviate teachers' professional responsibility to weigh carefully the various aspects of that evidence in determining the mark or grade that best summarizes students' achievement or performance. Computers do mathematical operations with great precision. Nevertheless, they do not lessen the obligation of educators to ensure that the marks or grades they assign are accurate, honest, and fair summaries of the quality of students' performances.

7

. . . .

Making Improvements in
Grading and Reporting

So far we've discussed what's involved in grading and reporting, the importance of purpose, and the need for comprehensive reporting systems. We now turn to our main goal: the important role that you, as a parent, play in grading and reporting. In particular, we focus on the important part you play in improvement efforts. To bring about positive and productive changes in grading and reporting, parents and educators must work together. Both have to do their part to initiate change, shape improvements, and assist in implementation.

In this chapter we'll consider specific things you can do to help in this process. First, specific steps you can take in working with teachers to improve communication between school and home will be outlined. Next, several important things you can do in working with your child to make reporting more effective and more helpful will be described. Finally, we'll examine the importance of gradual change in improvement efforts and the crucial role you can have in ensuring that planned improvements succeed.

Working with Teachers

Throughout this book it has been stressed that grading and reporting are more a challenge in effective communication than simply a task of documenting students' achievement. We've also emphasized that both parents and teachers share responsibilities in this process. Admittedly, most of the work in grading and reporting falls squarely on the shoulders of teachers. They're the ones who have to gather evidence on students' learning, evaluate that evidence, and then summarize and report the results of their evaluations. Still, parents have a vital role as well.

If, as a parent or guardian, you're going to be an active partner with educators in making improvements, you first must be knowledgeable of the issues involved in grading and reporting. Earlier chapters in this book were designed to help you gain that knowledge. But second, you have to take specific steps to make sure your involvement is positive and constructive. Several of the most important steps you can take are outlined here. Although these are not the only steps that might be helpful in making improvements, they are some of the most crucial.

Become Familiar with School Policies on Grading and Reporting

The first step in improving grading and reporting is to learn about district or school grading policies. Most schools today have established policies on grading that are outlined in district documents or faculty handbooks and are available to parents on request. Consequently, you'll have to ask a school official for a copy. Once you get it, read the policy carefully and make sure you understand it. Although most school grading policies are quite general, they provide the basis from which improvement efforts must build.

School-level policies often stipulate the format of report cards, the frequency of progress reports, and the schedule of parent-teacher conferences. Changes in these reporting tools therefore have to be initiated at the school level. In some cases established school grading policies pose barriers to better practice and must be changed immediately. Some grading policies, for example, specify the inclusion of nonacademic factors such as punctuality or absenteeism in determining students' grades. Others stipulate the use of averaging to obtain final course grades. Unsound policies such as these must be revised before other, more significant improvements become possible.

Learn About Teachers' Grading Policies and Practices

The general nature of most district and school grading policies allows individual teachers great latitude in determining the details of their classroom grading practices. The next step in improving grading and reporting therefore is to become familiar with teachers' grading policies. These are, after all, the policies that most directly affect your child.

Many teachers go out of their way to inform parents about their grading policies, so gaining this information is seldom a problem. Some teachers use open-house meetings to tell parents about how they determine students' grades. At the same time many will describe how they plan to keep parents up-to-date on their child's learning progress. Middle and secondary teachers frequently distribute written statements that describe their grading procedures and how they combine various aspects of students' performance to calculate course grades. Occasionally teachers post their grading policies on classroom Web sites.

Most teachers also welcome parents' questions about their grading policies and practices. But how you pose your questions is extremely important. If teachers feel that your questions challenge their honesty or professional judgment, they may react defensively. Asking, for example, "How did you come up with this grade?" or, "Is this truly the grade you think this assignment deserves?" inevitably makes the discussion confrontational. But when teachers believe that your questions stem from a genuine interest in understanding their grading policies, they tend to be much more open and receptive. Questions such as, "Can you help me understand how you arrived at this grade?" or, "Can you tell me what you were looking for in this assignment?" usually lead to more pleasant and informative discussions.

In addition, you shouldn't hesitate to ask your child's teachers for specific suggestions about how grades on future assignments or assessments might be improved. And "specific" is the key word here. Don't be satisfied with vague responses such as "Study more," "Be more conscientious," or "Try harder." Instead, press for detailed and prescriptive information that you can use to guide changes in your child's activities at home and in school. Again, when teachers realize that the request is coming from a parent with a sincere interest in helping their child do better, they're usually quite willing to offer explicit advice. Most teachers will also notify you when they notice improvements in your child's performance.

Actively Participate in All Reporting Activities

One of the greatest frustrations teachers report in grading and reporting is the lack of parent interest and participation. Therefore, one of the most important steps you can take to improve grading and reporting is to become an active participant in all reporting activities. In most cases this doesn't require a lot of extra time or energy. What it does require, however, is doing a few small things regularly in order to become a full partner with educators in the reporting process.

Being an active participant in reporting activities means regularly attending open house meetings, parent-teacher conferences, and student-led conferences. Despite your many other responsibilities, you have to make your child's education a priority. It also means showing up at these meetings on time and staying until all activities are completed. And don't forget to take along a pen and paper to make notes about the things you will want to discuss later with your child. If for any reason you're unable to attend at the scheduled time, make other arrangements to visit the school and meet with your child's teacher at a time that's mutually convenient.

To keep abreast of what's going on in school you also must take the time to read any materials your child brings home from school. Go over report cards, papers, and other samples of classroom work with your child to check on learning progress and to make sure the teacher's expectations are understood. Be sure to read school and class newsletters carefully. Regularly respond to surveys, question-naires, and notes that are sent home from school officials. Time per-mitting, you might volunteer to serve on school committees and take part in parent training programs.

Most important, don't hesitate to contact your child's teacher when questions or concerns arise about school-related matters. Major learning problems often begin as minor difficulties that were left unattended. For this reason, you should get in touch with the teacher as soon as a problem is identified so that immediate steps can be taken to find a solution. In addition, be sure to notify the teacher of events outside of school that might affect your child's work. Knowing, for example, about a separation or divorce, the death of a family member, or a change in job that might alter your time at home can help teachers address accompanying learning problems much more efficiently.

To honor teachers' privacy, it's best to contact them during school hours through a note, phone call, or e-mail. After discussing the problem, be sure to follow through with any suggestions the teacher makes and keep track of the changes made. You might also request a follow-up phone call or meeting with the teacher to make sure that the problem has been resolved.

Discuss Concerns over Grading Issues Directly with Teachers

Sometimes parents read every report from school, communicate fre-quently with teachers, remain involved in their child's education, but still have occasional concerns about the school's or an individual teacher's grading policies. In such instances, you shouldn't hesitate to contact the teacher directly, again at a time that honors the teacher's privacy. Too often parents remain silent when such issues arise, fearing that the teacher will be offended by their questions and concerns and perhaps take it out on their child. But teachers need to know about such concerns and generally appreciate polite, honest, and direct communication. Raising the issue might help the teacher recognize an unanticipated problem that affects many students.

If the teacher does not respond or appears uncooperative, then you should request an appointment with the school principal to discuss your concern. Positive and productive change efforts often begin with thoughtful requests from parents. It's important, however, to recognize the "chain of command" in schools and to contact the teacher first before moving to the principal or higher-level administrators. Problems or concerns that can be resolved at the class level need go no further unless larger, schoolwide issues are involved.

Steps in Working with Teachers to Improve Grading and Reporting

1. Become familiar with school policies on grading and reporting.
2. Learn about teachers' grading policies and practices.
3. Actively participate in all reporting activities.
4. Discuss concerns over grading issues directly with teachers.

Working with Children

Parents have a powerful influence on their children's attitudes toward school, learning, and particularly grades. Unfortunately, most don't know how best to take advantage of that influence. Few parents take the time to discuss grading and reporting with their children. Some, in fact, unconsciously avoid discussions about grades because it brings back memories of their own bad experiences. They recall the disappointment they felt after receiving a low grade for a class project because the teacher's expectations were unclear. Others remember their embarrassment in being identified as the student who "earned" the lowest grade in the class—an event that ranks right next to being the last one chosen for a team in gym class. By steering clear of discussions about grades, these parents hope to save their children similar disappointment and embarrassment. Unfortunately, it never works.

Conversations between you and your child about grading and reporting are vitally important. They provide an opportunity for you to show your interest in school and learning. They also help children gain a better understanding of the purposes of different reporting tools. But most important, these discussions can help children develop a healthy attitude toward grading and reporting that will benefit them throughout their school years.

The following are several of the most important steps you can take to ensure these conversations remain positive and helpful. Although these, too, are not the only steps you can take, they represent an excellent starting point.

Emphasize the Importance of Grading and Reporting

Some parents today are afraid of putting too much emphasis grades. They remember the academic pressure they felt from their parents and don't want to subject their children to the same. So instead of emphasizing the importance of good grades, they give their children the message that "grades don't count as long as you're learning." Those who do, however, inevitably regret it. Their children soon begin refusing to commit themselves to doing the work or putting forth the effort necessary to earn high grades simply because "it's the learning that counts; not the grade." And, after all, they are learning some things (Rimm, 1995).

A better strategy is to take a more balanced approach in emphasizing the importance of grades. In discussions with your child about schoolwork you should emphasize that grades *are* important and that high grades or marks will require his or her best effort. But at the same time, you should stress the communication purposes of grading. Point out that report cards, progress reports, and parent-teacher conferences are all designed to let parents know how their children are doing in school. These and other reporting tools inform parents about their children's progress on learning tasks, in what areas they're doing well, and where additional help or assistance might be needed.

By emphasizing the communication purposes of grading and reporting you help your child see grades as a short-term appraisal rather than as a permanent label. Be sure to point out, for example, that grades or marks relate to a particular set of tasks performed at a particular time—and that things can change. Low grades or marks can be improved with additional work and effort. High grades similarly might drop if the quality of the work or effort decline.

Discuss Teachers' Grading Policies and Practices

Discussions between parents and their children about grading and reporting also should address individual teachers' grading practices. Children experience these practices on a daily basis and, hence, find such discussions immediately relevant. But in these conversations as well, it's important to emphasize the communication aspects of grading and reporting.

Children whose parents stress that the primary purpose of grades is to inform tend to focus on learning rather than on simply attaining a grade. Plus, these children are usually more willing to discuss their schoolwork with their parents. Children whose parents view grades as labels, on the other hand, often avoid discussions of their work in school, especially when they're experiencing problems or learning difficulties. To these children, a low grade or mark is an indication of incompetence or lack of ability, rather than a temporary setback that can be remedied. Not wanting to disappoint their parents, they steer clear of discussions about grades. Parents who initiate open and honest discussions with their children about teachers' grading policies keep open the avenues of communication and maintain a focus on learning progress.

Discuss Grades and Marks on a Regular Basis

Don't let grades and reporting be topics that you discuss with your child only when the report card comes home. Instead, include grades as part of the regular conversations you have with your child about schoolwork.

It's usually best to begin these discussions with a general question about what's going on in school. Asking, for example, "What are you reading in language arts?" or, "How's math going?" can initiate conversations that will help you keep up-to-date with your child's experiences in school and then lead naturally to the topic of grades. Similarly, asking about specific class activities and homework assignments, upcoming quizzes or tests, and class projects not only keeps you informed but also serves as a gentle reminder to your child of the importance of preparation.

How you respond to your child's marks or grades is also critically important. This is especially true when those grades are lower than you expected or hoped for. Children whose parents criticize or reprimand them for a low grade often become reluctant to share their experiences in school. They feel that it's better to say nothing and dodge, at least temporarily, their parents' disapproval. On the other hand, children whose parents treat a low grade as an indication that help is needed or a change in approach is required generally remain open to discussing school matters.

Even the tone you take in these discussions can have significant influence on your child. Asking, for example, "How did this happen?" or, "How did you do so terribly?" usually prompts a very different response from children than questions such as, "How can we improve this mark?" and, "What can we do to get a better grade next time?" Children need to know that you regard their grades seriously, but that you see grades as a temporary reflection of current work, not as a permanent and unalterable condition. They also need to know that you are on their side in whatever changes need to be made. It's not, "What are *you* going to do about this?" but rather, "What can *we* do to improve this grade?"

Children accustomed to talking with their parents about school and their grades are generally more comfortable sharing information, even when that information isn't good news. This is especially true if their parents have emphasized the communication purposes of grades. Regular conversations about grading also help avoid unwelcome surprises when the report card does come home.

Encourage Children to Ask Questions About Their Grades and What They Can Do to Improve

Most teachers today try to be clear about what they expect students to learn. The majority also take time to explain the criteria they plan to use in evaluating students' achievement or performance. But if for any reason these expectations or criteria remain unclear, students should not hesitate to ask their teachers for clarification.

Doing well in school requires that children understand what is expected of them. And since grades, in large part, are based on the teacher's expectations, children need to know what those expectations are. This doesn't mean that a grade should be questioned just because it's lower than anticipated. However, you should encourage your child to ask the teacher to explain what is expected in an assignment or learning assessment if those expectations are unclear, and also what steps he or she might take to improve performance in the future.

Recognize Both Achievement and Improvement

Children truly value their parents' recognition, and most will do just about anything to gain it. That's why it's so important for you to recognize your child's achievements in school and make special note of improvements. Children whose parents let them know that their academic accomplishments are important and valued tend to persist in their efforts to do well and often attain very high levels of achievement.

Always remember, however, that *recognizing* is different from *rewarding*. Some parents offer their children money for high grades or promise special rewards for attaining a certain grade average. But despite their good intentions, practices such as these may do more harm than good. In some cases they cause children to put more value on the reward than on the learning. Instead of taking pride in their accomplishments as learners, they focus on the grade itself and what it will bring them.

Good grades and improvements in school performance can certainly be celebrated. A special visit to the zoo, a movie, or a trip to the ice cream parlor in honor of a good report card is an excellent way to recognize a child's accomplishments. But to most children, their parents' praise and open expression of pride in their effort and hard work are more important than any of these celebratory events.

Treat Low Grades as a Signal of Needed Change, Not as a Reason for Punishment

Regardless of their child's skills and talents, most parents have to contend with at least occasional low grades. How you deal with this can have a powerful influence on your child's efforts in school and the relationship you and your child share.

Above all, low grades shouldn't be treated as a reason for punishment. As we mentioned earlier, doing so inevitably results in increased reluctance in children to discuss schoolwork with their parents. Instead, a low grade should be treated as a signal that additional work and effort are needed. In particular, a low grade points out where past performance hasn't been in line with the teacher's expectations and a change in preparation strategies is required.

Children of all ages need to understand that their actions have consequences, of course. And the consequence of a low grade may mean that certain restrictions will be imposed. Children may, for instance, be required to attend special after-school study sessions until improvements are evident. Others may be required to spend a particular amount of time studying each evening before turning on the television or playing video games. Although some children may consider such restrictions to be a form of punishment, these actions are actually well-targeted and purposeful corrective strategies. Rather than simply denying children something they enjoy, these restrictions allow for more time and greater commitment to schoolwork so that performance can be improved. Teachers should be consulted, too, for additional recommendations or actions that could bring improvements.

Most important, parents must be willing to do their part when imposing these restrictions. For example, you may have to make sure your child has a quiet place to study, even if only the kitchen table. This might mean turning off a television program you normally watch so that your child can work without distraction or interruption. Although actions such as these may disrupt your evening routine, they show your child that you regard learning and schoolwork as important. It also allows you to be available to your child if questions or concerns about the work arise.

Steps in Working with Children to Improve Achievement

1. Emphasize the importance of grading and reporting
2. Discuss teachers' grading policies and practices
3. Discuss grades and marks on a regular basis
4. Encourage children to ask questions about their grades and what they can do to improve
5. Recognize both achievement and improvement
6. Treat low grades as a signal of needed change, not as a reason for punishment

---

Gradual Change Strategies

Improving grading and reporting requires change. And though change is never easy, when it comes to grading and reporting, the process can be downright painful. Long-held traditions guide so much of what is done in grading and reporting that even modest changes can be difficult to implement.

Successful efforts to improve grading and reporting typically adhere to two general guidelines. The first is to "Think big, but start small" (Guskey, 1995). When it comes to grading and reporting, everything can't be accomplished at once. Meaningful and productive change takes time. Therefore, improvements have to be made gradually, allowing time to address problems and concerns that arise along the way.

To "think big" means focusing on a reporting system and all of the different ways information about student learning can be communicated. In other words, educators and parents must share a grand vision for what needs to be accomplished. This, in turn, requires consideration of the wide variety of reporting tools available, how each tool can be used most efficiently, and how different tools can be combined in a well-organized and effective reporting system.

To "start small" means recognizing that not everything can be changed immediately. Improvement efforts might begin, for example, with the addition of a few, new reporting tools that haven't been used in the past. Student-led conference, Friday folders, or a schedule of regular phone calls might be initiated to encourage more open communication between educators and parents. Input from teachers, parents, and students can be used to refine these reporting tools and to enhance collaboration among all those who have a stake in the process.

With these changes in place, attention might then turn to the more challenging task of revising the report card or other established reporting tools. Care should be taken to ensure that the revisions are based on available research evidence and an established knowledge base. In other words, educators and parents need to investigate what reliable educational research has to say about these various reporting tools. Findings from relevant studies and information from schools that have implemented successful changes in grading and reporting should be thoroughly considered.

The second guideline evident in successful improvement efforts is to ensure that all work begins by clarifying purposes. What information do we want to communicate? Who is the primary audience for that information? How will that information be used? These questions need to be addressed before any new reporting tool is added or any established tool revised. Clarifying purposes keeps everyone headed in the right direction. It also makes it easier to judge the effectiveness of the changes made.

Improvements in grading and reporting seldom come easily. But those that are thoughtful and well informed, made gradually, and implemented with a clear sense of purpose can yield important advantages to educators, parents, and students.

Conclusion

Grading, by its very nature, is a subjective process. It involves one group of human beings (teachers) making judgments about the performance of another group of human beings (students) and communicating those judgments to a third group of human beings (parents). But as discussed early on, being subjective doesn't mean that the process lacks credibility or is indefensible. Rather, it simply implies that grading is and will always be an exercise in professional judgment and related communication.

Above all, grading and reporting require careful planning and a clear focus on purpose. When done well, they are based on honesty, fairness, and an overriding concern for students' well-being. Such qualities ensure that parents will be provided with high-quality information on their children's learning, regardless of the method used. They also ensure that the results will be beneficial to students, regardless of the level of education involved. Working together, parents and educators can make grading and reporting an effective and highly successful process.

References

Abou-Sayf, F. K. (1996). An investigation of different grading practices: Reliability, validity, and related psychometric considerations. *Journal of Applied Research in the Community College, 4*(1), 39–47.

Adelman, C. (1999). *Answers in the tool box: Academic intensity, attendance patterns, and bachelor's degree attainment.* Washington, DC: Office of Educational Research and Improvement, U.S. Department of Education.

Afflerbach, P., and Sammons, R. B. (1991). *Report cards in literacy evaluation: Teachers' training, practices, and values.* Paper presented at the annual meeting of the National Reading Conference, Palm Springs, CA.

Agnew, E. (1993). *Department grade quotas: The silent saboteur.* Paper presented at the annual meeting of the Conference on College Composition and Communication, San Diego, CA.

Agnew, E. (1995). Rigorous grading does not raise standards: It only lowers grades. *Assessing Writing, 2*(1), 91–103.

Allison, E., and Friedman, S. J. (1995). Reforming report cards. *Executive Educator, 17*(1), 38–39.

Andrade, H. G. (2000). Using rubrics to promote thinking and learning. *Educational Leadership, 57*(5), 13–18.

Arter, J. A., and McTighe, J. (2001). *Scoring rubrics in the classroom.* Thousand Oaks, CA: Corwin.

Arter, J. A., and Spandel, V. (1992). Using portfolios of student work in instruction and assessment (ITEMS module). *Educational Measurement: Issues and Practice, 12*(1), 36–44.

Austin, S., and McCann, R. (1992). *"Here's another arbitrary grade for your collection": A statewide study of grading policies.* Paper presented at the annual meeting of the American Educational Research Association, San Francisco.

Bailey, J. M., and Guskey, T. R. (2001). *Implementing student-led conferences*. Thousand Oaks, CA: Corwin.

Balm, S.S.M. (1995). Using portfolio assessment in a kindergarten classroom. *Teaching and Change, 2*(2), 141–151.

Barnes, L.L.B., Bull, K. S., Perry, K., and Campbell, N. J. (1998). *Discipline-related differences in teaching and grading philosophies among undergraduate teaching faculty*. Paper presented at the annual meeting of the American Educational Research Association, San Diego, CA.

Barnes, S. (1985). A study of classroom pupil evaluation: The missing link in teacher education. *Journal of Teacher Education, 36*(4), 46–49.

Barton, P. (1999). *Too much testing of the wrong kind, too little of the right kind in K–12 education*. Princeton, NJ: Educational Testing Service.

Basinger, D. (1997). Fighting grade inflation: A misguided effort? *College Teaching, 45*(3), 88–91.

Beaver, W. (1997). Declining college standards: It's not the courses, it's the grades. *College Board Review, 181*, 2–7.

Berg, M. H., and Smith, J. P. (1996). Using videotapes to improve teaching. *Music Educators' Journal, 82*(4), 31–37.

Bishop, J. H. (1992). Why U.S. students need incentives to learn. *Educational Leadership, 49*(6), 15–18.

Bloom, B. S., Madaus, G. F., and Hastings, J. T. (1981). *Evaluation to improve learning*. New York: McGraw-Hill.

Bracey, G. W. (1994). Grade inflation? *Phi Delta Kappan, 76*(4), 328–329.

Bracey, G. W. (1998). More about grade inflation or lack of it. *Phi Delta Kappan, 79*(8), 629–630.

Bracey, G. W. (1999). Getting that sheepskin. *Phi Delta Kappan, 81*(2), 169–170.

Brewer, W. R., and Kallick, B. (1996). Technology's promise for reporting student learning. In T. R. Guskey (Ed.), *Communicating student learning. 1996 yearbook of the Association for Supervision and Curriculum Development* (pp. 178–187). Alexandria, VA: Association for Supervision and Curriculum Development.

Brookhart, S. M. (1991). Grading practices and validity. *Educational Measurement: Issues and Practice, 10*(1), 35–36.

Brookhart, S. M. (1993). Teachers' grading practices: Meaning and values. *Journal of Educational Measurement, 30*(2), 123–142.

Brookhart, S. M. (1999). Teaching about communicating assessment results and grading. *Educational Measurement: Issues and Practice, 18*(1), 5–13.

Cameron, J., and Pierce, W. D. (1994). Reinforcement, reward, and intrinsic motivation: A meta-analysis. *Review of Educational Research, 64*(3), 363–423.

Cameron, J., and Pierce, W. D. (1996). The debate about rewards and intrinsic motivation: Protests and accusations do not alter the results. *Review of Educational Research, 66*(1), 39–51.

Canady, R. L., and Hotchkiss, P. R. (1989). It's a good score! Just a bad grade. *Phi Delta Kappan, 71*(1), 68–71.

Cattermole, J., and Robinson, N. (1985). Effective home/school communication—from the parents' perspective. *Phi Delta Kappan, 67*(1), 48–50.

Chang, L. (1993). *Using confirmatory factor analysis of multitrait-multimethod data to assess the psychometrical equivalence of 4-point and 6-point Likert-type scales.* Paper presented at the annual meeting of the National Council on Measurement in Education, Atlanta.

Chang, L. (1994). A psychometric evaluation of 4-point and 6-point Likert-type scales in relation to reliability and validity. *Applied Psychological Measurement, 18*(3), 205–215.

Chastain, K. (1990). Characteristics of graded and ungraded compositions. *Modern Language Journal, 74*(1), 10–14.

Chrispeels, J., Fernandez, B., and Preston, J. (1991). *Home and school partners in student success: A handbook for principals and staff.* San Diego, CA: San Diego City Schools Community Relations and Integration Services Division.

Cooper, H. (1989). Synthesis of research on homework. *Educational Leadership, 47*(3), 85–91.

Cooper, H. (2001). *The battle over homework: An administrator's guide to setting sound and effective policies* (2nd ed.). Thousand Oaks, CA: Corwin.

Cross, L. H., and Frary, R. B. (1996). *Hodgepodge grading: Endorsed by students and teachers alike.* Paper presented at the annual meeting of the National Council on Measurement in Education, New York.

Davies, A. (1996). *Student-centered assessment and evaluation.* Merville, British Columbia: Classroom Connections International.

Davies, A. (2000). Seeing the results for yourself: A portfolio primer. *Classroom Leadership, 3*(5), 4–5.

Dwyer, C. A. (1996). Cut scores and testing: Statistics, judgment, truth, and error. *Psychological Assessment, 8*(4), 360–362.

Eastwood, K. W. (1996). Reporting student progress: One district's attempt with student literacy. In T. R. Guskey (Ed.), *Communicating student learning.*

1996 yearbook of the Association for Supervision and Curriculum Development (pp. 65–78). Alexandria, VA: Association for Supervision and Curriculum Development.

Ebel, R. L. (1979). *Essentials of educational measurement* (3rd ed.). Upper Saddle River, NJ: Prentice Hall.

Farley, B. L. (1995). "A" is for average: The grading crisis in today's colleges. In *Issues of education at community colleges: Essays by fellows in the Mid-Career Fellowship Program at Princeton University.* Princeton, NJ: Princeton University Press. (ERIC Document Reproduction Service No. ED384384)

Feldman, A., Kropf, A., and Alibrand, M. (1996). *Making grades: How high school science teachers determine report card grades.* Paper presented at the annual meeting of the American Educational Research Association, New York.

Feldmesser, R. A. (1971). *The positive functions of grades.* Paper presented at the annual meeting of the American Educational Research Association, New York.

Frary, R. B., Cross, L. H., and Weber, L. J. (1993). Testing and grading practices and opinions of secondary teachers of academic subjects: Implications for instruction in measurement. *Educational Measurement: Issues and Practice, 12*(3), 23–30.

Friedman, S. J., and Frisbie, D. A. (1995). The influence of report cards on the validity of grades reported to parents. *Educational and Psychological Measurement, 55*(1), 5–26.

Friedman, S. J., Valde, G. A., and Obermeyer, B. J. (1998). Computerized report card comment menus: Teacher use and teacher-parent perceptions. *Michigan Principal, 74*(3), 11–14, 21.

Frisbie, D. A., and Waltman, K. K. (1992). Developing a personal grading plan. *Educational Measurement: Issues and Practices, 11*(3), 35–42.

Galen, H. (1994). Developmentally appropriate practice: Myths and facts. *Principal, 73*(5), 20–22.

Giba, M. A. (1999). Forging partnerships between parents and teachers. *Principal, 78*(3), 33–35.

Gilman, D. A., and Swan, E. (1989). Solving GPA and class rank problems. *NASSP Bulletin, 73*(515), 91–97.

Gitomer, D. H., and Pearlman, M. A. (1999). Are teacher licensing tests too easy? Are standards too low? *ETS Developments, 45*(1), 4–5.

Gose, B. (1997, March 21). Duke rejects controversial plan to revise calculation of grade point averages. *Chronicle of Higher Education,* p. A53.

Gray, K. (1993). Why we will lose: Taylorism in America's high schools. *Phi Delta Kappan, 74*(5), 370–374.

Greenwood, T. W. (1995). Let's turn on the VCR and watch your report card. *Principal, 74*(4), 48–49.

Guskey, T. R. (1993). Should letter grades be abandoned? *ASCD Update, 35*(7), 7.

Guskey, T. R. (1994). Making the grade: What benefits students. *Educational Leadership, 52*(2), 14–20.

Guskey, T. R. (1995). Professional development in education: In search of the optimal mix. In T. R. Guskey and M. Huberman (Eds.), *Professional development education: New paradigms and practices* (pp. 114–131). New York: Teachers College Press.

Guskey, T. R. (Ed.). (1996). *Communicating student learning. 1996 yearbook of the Association for Supervision and Curriculum Development.* Alexandria, VA: Association for Supervision and Curriculum Development.

Guskey, T. R. (1997). *Implementing mastery learning* (2nd ed.). Belmont, CA: Wadsworth.

Guskey, T. R., (1999, April 1). Inflation not the issue; focus on grades' purpose. *Lexington Herald-Leader*, p. A-19.

Guskey, T. R. (2000). Grading policies that work against standards . . . and how to fix them. *NASSP Bulletin, 84*(620), 20–29.

Guskey, T. R. (2001). High percentages are not the same as high standards. *Phi Delta Kappan, 82*(7), 534–536.

Guskey, T. R., and Bailey, J. (2001). *Developing grading and reporting systems for student learning.* Thousand Oaks, CA: Corwin.

Gustafson, C. (1998). Phone home. *Educational Leadership, 56*(2), 31–32.

Haladyna, T. M. (1999). *A complete guide to student grading.* Needham Heights, MA: Allyn & Bacon.

Hall, K. (1990). *Determining the success of narrative report cards.* (ERIC Document Reproduction Service No. ED334013)

Hargis, C. H. (1990). *Grades and grading practices.* Springfield, IL: Thomas.

Henderson, A., and Berla, A. (1995). *A new generation of evidence: Family involvement is critical to students' achievement.* Columbia, MD: National Committee for Citizens in Education.

Hills, J. R. (1983). Interpreting grade-equivalent scores. *Educational Measurement: Issues and Practice, 2*(1), 15, 21.

Hills, J. R. (1991). Apathy concerning grading and testing. *Phi Delta Kappan, 72*(7), 540–545.

Hoover-Dempsey, K. V., and Sandler, H. M. (1997). Why do parents become involved in their children's education? *Review of Educational Research, 67*(1), 3–42.

Huber, J. (1997). Gradebook programs: Which ones make the grade? *Technology Connection, 4*(1), 21–23.

Johnson, D. W., and Johnson, R. T. (1989). *Cooperation and competition: Theory and research*. Edina, MN: Interaction.

Johnson, D. W., Skon, L., and Johnson, R. T. (1980). Effects of cooperative, competitive, and individualistic conditions on children's problem-solving performance. *American Educational Research Journal, 17*(1), 83–93.

Johnson, R. T., Johnson, D. W., and Tauer, M. (1979). The effects of cooperative, competitive, and individualistic goal structures on students' attitudes and achievement. *Journal of Psychology, 102*, 191–198.

Kirschenbaum, H. (1999). Night and day: Succeeding with parents at School 43. *Principal, 78*(3), 20–23.

Kovas, M. A. (1993). Make your grading motivating: Keys to performance based evaluation. *Quill and Scroll, 68*(1), 10–11.

Kreider, H. M., and Lopez, M. E. (1999). Promising practices for family involvement. *Principal, 78*(3), 16–19.

Krumboltz, J. D., and Yeh, C. J. (1996). Competitive grading sabotages good teaching. *Phi Delta Kappan, 78*(4), 324–326.

Kwon, I. G., and Kendig, N. L. (1997). Grade inflation from a career counselor's perspective. *Journal of Employment Counseling, 34*(2), 50–54.

Langdon, C. A. (1999). The fifth Phi Delta Kappa poll of teachers' attitudes toward the public schools. *Phi Delta Kappan, 80*(8), 611–618.

Libit, H. (1999). Report card redux. *School Administrator, 56*(10), 6–10.

Linn, R. L. (1983). Testing and instruction: Links and distinctions. *Journal of Educational Measurement, 20*(2), 179–189.

Little, A. W., and Allan, J. (1989). Student-led parent-teacher conferences. *Elementary School Guidance and Counseling, 23*(3), 210–218.

Lockhart, E. (1990). Heavy grades? A study on weighted grades. *Journal of College Admission, 126*, 9–16.

McMillan, J. H. (2001). Essential assessment concepts for teachers and administrators. Thousand Oaks, CA: Corwin.

McMillan, J. H., Workman, D., and Myran, S. (1999). *Elementary teachers' classroom assessment and grading practices*. Paper presented at the annual meeting of the American Educational Research Association, Montreal.

Million, J. (1999). Restaurants, report cards, and reality. *NAESP Communicator, 22*(8), 5, 7.

Mitchell, B. M. (1994). Weighted grades. *Gifted Child Today, 17*(4), 28–29.

Nelson, K. (2000). Measuring the intangibles. *Classroom Leadership, 3*(5), 1, 8.

Nitko, A. J., and Niemierko, B. (1993). *Qualitative letter grade standards for teacher-made summative classroom assessments*. Paper presented at the annual meeting of the American Educational Research Association, Atlanta.

O'Connor, K. (1999). *How to grade for learning*. Arlington Heights, IL: Skylight.

O'Donnell, A., and Woolfolk, A. E. (1991). *Elementary and secondary teachers' beliefs about testing and grading*. Paper presented at the annual meeting of the American Psychological Association, San Francisco.

Ornstein, A. C. (1994). Grading practices and policies: An overview and some suggestions. *NASSP Bulletin, 78*(559), 55–64.

Pardini, P. (1997). Report card reform. *School Administrator, 54*(11), 19–25.

Payne, D. A. (1974). *The assessment of learning*. Lexington, MA: Heath.

Polloway, E. A., Epstein, M. H., Bursuck, W. D., Roderique, T. W., McConeghy, J. L., and Jayanthi, M. (1994). Classroom grading: A national survey of policies. *Remedial and Special Education, 15*(2), 162–170.

Rich, D. (1998). What parents want from teachers. *Educational Leadership, 55*(3), 37–39.

Rimm, S. (1995). *Why bright kids get poor grades—and what you can do about it*. New York: Three Rivers Press.

Robinson, D. (1998). Student portfolios in mathematics. *Mathematics Teacher, 91*(4), 318–325.

Schulz, H. W. (1999). *Reporting student progress, grades, and the role of parent-teacher conferences*. Paper presented at the annual meeting of the American Educational Research Association, Montreal.

Stiggins, R. J. (1993). Teacher training in assessment: Overcoming the neglect. In S. L. Wise (Ed.), *Teacher training in measurement and assessment skills* (pp. 27–40). Lincoln, NE: Buros Institute of Mental Measurements.

Stiggins, R. J. (2001). Report cards. In R. J. Stiggins, *Student-involved classroom assessment* (3rd ed., pp. 409–466). Upper Saddle River, NJ: Merrill Prentice Hall.

Talley, N. R., and Mohr, J. I. (1991). Weighted averages, computer screening, and college admission in public colleges and universities. *Journal of College Admission, 132*, 9–11.

Tomlinson, T. (1992). *Hard work and high expectations: Motivating students to learn*. Washington, DC: Office of Educational Research and Improvement, U.S. Department of Education.

Truog, A. L., and Friedman, S. J. (1996). *Evaluating high school teachers' written grading policies from a measurement perspective*. Paper presented at the annual meeting of the National Council on Measurement in Education, New York.

Vockell, E. L., and Fiore, D. J. (1993). Electronic gradebooks: What current programs can do for teachers. *Clearing House*, 66(3), 141–145.

Waltman, K. K., and Frisbie, D. A. (1994). Parents' understanding of their children's report card grades. *Applied Measurement in Education*, 7(3), 223–240.

Watts, K. H. (1996). Bridges freeze before roads. In T. R. Guskey (Ed.), *Communicating student learning: 1996 yearbook of the Association for Supervision and Curriculum Development* (pp. 6–12). Alexandria, VA: Association for Supervision and Curriculum Development.

Wiggins, G. (1994). Toward better report cards. *Educational Leadership*, 52(2), 28–35.

Wiggins, G. (1996). Honesty and fairness: Toward better grading and reporting. In T. R. Guskey (Ed.), *Communicating student learning: 1996 yearbook of the Association for Supervision and Curriculum Development* (pp. 141–176). Alexandria, VA: Association for Supervision and Curriculum Development.

Wiggins, G. (1997). Tips on reforming student report cards. *School Administrator*, 54(11), 20.

Wiggins, G., and McTighe, J. (1998). *Understanding by design*. Alexandria, VA: Association for Supervision and Curriculum Development.

Willis, S. (1993). Are letter grades obsolete? *ASCD Update*, 35(7), 1, 4, 8.

Wright, R. G. (1994). Success for all: The median is the key. *Phi Delta Kappan*, 75(9), 723–725.

Zirkel, P. A. (1995, March 8). Grade inflation: A problem and a proposal. *Education Week*, p. 28.

The Author

· ·

Thomas R. Guskey is professor of educational policy studies and evaluation at the University of Kentucky. He has taught at all school levels, worked as a school administrator in the Chicago Public Schools, and was the first director of the Center for the Improvement of Teaching and Learning, a national educational research center. He is a regular presenter at national educational conferences, has served as consultant to educators in every state and several foreign countries, and was recently featured in a special segment on National Public Radio. He is author of many award-winning books and articles that bring clarity to some of education's most complex problems. Most important, he is a struggling but caring and very proud parent.

Index

on, 30–31; types of, 29–30. *See also*
Criterion-referenced standards;
Norm-referenced standards; Process
criteria; Product criteria; Progress
criteria
Criterion-referenced standards: clarifying, 28–31; defined, 2, 27; for letter grade descriptors, 44–45;
norm-referenced standards *versus*,
27–28, 73–74; research supporting,
27–28. *See also* Process criteria;
Product criteria; Progress criteria;
Standards-based grading
Cross, L. H., 30, 45
CTB/McGraw-Hill, 51
Cultural barriers, 90
Curve, grading on. *See* Norm-referenced standards
Cutoffs: challenge of, 79–80; issues of,
76–81; for letter grades, 45–46; levels of challenge and, 76–79, 80–81;
for percentage grades, 55, 76–81;
recommendations about, 80–81

D

Davies, A., 99, 103
Description, grading for, 3
Descriptive information, combined
with points-based information, 23
Descriptive narratives. *See* Narratives
Descriptors: for letter grades, 43–45;
performance-level, for standards-
based grading, 59, 61
Detail, level of: categorical grades
and, 53; letter grades and, 46; narratives and, 67, 68–69; parents'
preferences for, 14, 49–50, 55; plus
and minus letter grades and, 48–50;
standards-based grading and,
68–69; subjectivity and, 26; value
of, for students, 26
"Developing," 51
"Developmentally appropriate,"
meaning of, to parents, 14–15
Diagnosis, checking for, 3
Digital portfolios, 107

Disadvantaged students, 31
"Distinguished," 51
Dwyer, C. A., 48

E

Early childhood, assessment in, 20
Eastwood, K. W., 106
Ebel, R. L., 7
Eddie Haskell Effect, 22
Educational growth, 29. *See also*
Progress criteria
Educational level(s): categorical
grades and, 51; grading inconsis-
tency across, 4; influence of, on
teachers' perceptions of grading,
17–18; letter grades and, 42; percentage grades and, 54; standards-
based grading and, 62
Effort: points for, 22; as process criteria, 36
Electronic gradebooks, 17, 107–111;
advantages of, 107; educational levels that use, 107; shortcomings of,
107–111; tallying methods in,
108–111
E-mail, 98, 102
Elementary school: categorical grades
for, 51; failing grades in, 53; homework in, 101; standards-based grading in, 62; verbal feedback in, 20;
video report cards in, 106
Elementary teachers, perceptions of,
about grading, 17
Emerging, meaning of, to parents, 14
"Emerging," 51
Evaluated projects and assignments,
98–99
Evaluation of instructional program,
grades used for, 7, 8
Evidence: for checking *versus* grading,
3; relating purpose to, 38–39;
sources of, 31–38; using multiple
sources of, 32
Examinations: as process criteria, 32;
as product criteria, 32
"Excellent," 43, 44